# COURAGE TO CHANGE

## A PARADIGM FOR SUCCESS

**By Shirley Summer**

# COURAGE TO CHANGE
*A Paradigm for Success*

By Shirley Summer

Published By Summertime Press
Davis, California

First Edition 1993

ISBN: 0-9635039-3-6

**HOW TO ORDER**

Please submit all orders and correspondence to Communication Unlimited, P.O. Box 6405, Santa Maria, CA 93456; Telephone: (805) 937-8711/FAX (805) 937-3035

---

Book and Cover Design/Typesetting
ONE-ON-ONE Book Productions
Carolyn Porter, Todd Meisler, West Hills CA.

# Table of Contents

**To my Mother...**

who gave me her gift of strength and courage.

**To my Father...**

who taught me about love and patience—and heaven on earth.

# ACKNOWLEDGMENTS

It is important to me to express my thanks to the many people who have supported, loved, guided, and believed in me as I tackled this project. Each has given freely. Without these *earthly angels*, the book would not have happened.

Thank you to my many teachers and especially:

* Dr. Maria Nemeth, who spearheaded my change. I thank her for her rigorous coaching and for creating my first new family of friends.

* Dr. Siri Gian Singh Khalsa, who taught me about breathing, relaxing and letting change happen with gentleness and love.

* John Ruskell, who kept me in a state of questioning—always seeking higher truths.

* To Dr. Barbara Ruth Klein for genuinely sharing gifts of music and love. With her skillful guidance, I learned about the subtle changes of life through harmony, balance and beauty of song.

A grateful thank you to my friends and colleagues:

* Bob Bone, who never wavered in his belief in me. Thanks for being in my life.

* Kit Snyder, whose guidance, encouragement and support kept me going when I wanted to stop.

* To Sondra Olson, Shannon Eddy, Marjorie Salvesen for their contribution as readers. I

acknowledge their determination to live life fully.

❖ To Mary Spencer, for her dedication, friendship and keeping me on track.

❖ To my grown sons, Daron and Damon Whittle, who really never quite knew what I was up to... yet always trusted and believed in me. Thanks for the love and playtime!

❖ To Carolyn Porter and Todd Meisler of ONE-ON-ONE Book Productions for the final touches and look of the book.

And finally, thank you to Gordon Burgett and Susan Smily:

❖ To Gordon for his inspiration, sharing, and friendship. I couldn't have had a better mentor.

❖ To Susan for her courage, commitment, and willingness to do whatever it took to get the job done.

These people are angels in my life. I love you all.

*Shirley Summer*

# INTRODUCTION

*The Promise*
*The Process*
*The Paradigm for Change—Six Steps*
*Understanding How to Look at Change*

> Allow light to shine through to areas
> of your life where there is darkness;
> to the areas where you feel
> you have no choice.

## THE PROMISE

This book is written to help you look at yourself in a way that impacts you from the inside out. It presents a six-step process for change and personal happiness.

The process is simple—though not necessarily easy. It allows the present to happen without blame, reasons, excuses or making anyone wrong. You will experience new choices.

> Be ready for anything.
> Be unique — dare to be different!
> Everyone is original as long as he tells the truth.

## THE PROCESS

This process is a blend of body, mind and spirit. It is an examination of where you've been, where you are and where you're going. Part of the process is to examine the costs and benefits of change in terms of time, energy and money.

You will start out with a climb up the Mountain of Life—examining a metaphor for risking change. Then you will take an in-depth look at the six-step process of change. You will examine Time, Energy and Money; and the ways in which you deplete or renew your resources in each of these areas. Finally, you will consider the continuing process of change in your life.

## THE STILL, SMALL VOICE

*"Why am I here?" I asked.*
*I felt the discomfort*
*I felt the fear*
*I felt "This isn't it—"*

*And then I knew —*
*It's the quiet I seek*
*The quiet I must find*
*The quiet deep within.*

*Why am I here?*
*To settle, resolve and give up*
*Old, old ideas, beliefs and preconceptions*
*About the making of life.*

*To learn to love and be loved*
*Physically, emotionally, intellectually.*
*Listening to my body, listening to my heart*
*Learning what life is about:*

*Raindrops, roses, moonlight,*
*Kisses, caresses, hugs*
*Resting, reading, being.*

*To access the unconsciousness*
*For freedom of choice—*
*That's what life is about.*

3

> When you commit to change,
> it starts happening.

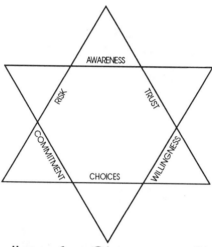

# The Paradigm for Change—Six Steps

1. The first step towards change is an AWARENESS of what is occuring around you, in your workplace, in your relationships, in your lives. It is a waking up to what is. It is simply noticing what is going on, like those little voices in your head that tell you:

   ☐ Life is hard ...

   ☐ They can't give me what I want ...

   ☐ If only I had ...

   ☐ I could have if ...

   Awareness is the first component of this paradigm for change.

2. A WILLINGNESS to be open to new ideas and concepts, to look at new and different possibilities, to leave the rut: this is the second step in breaking old

patterns. Once you are aware of these patterns, you can then ask yourself if you are willing to examine new possibilities, to consider living life in a different way.

3. Next comes COMMITMENT to do whatever it takes to get the job done. This is a dedication to a long term course of action. Whether it is an individual, a family or an organization making a commitment to change, it becomes necessary to give up previously held notions and concepts. It means making a decision. Commitment is important at any level of change—it takes you through your personal barriers.

4. Consider the RISKS taken daily by winning football or baseball teams. Think about investors who are willing to risk losing in order to win. Do you remember the first home or car you ever bought and how scared you were when you were making those decisions and signing that contract? Having the courage to change means risking. If nothing is risked, nothing is gained.

5. You must have TRUST in yourself. People who take risks have an ability to listen to their inner selves. You need to trust your decisions and act on them. You will find coaches who support you in reaching your dreams and visions. You may build a team of friends and associates who help and encourage you as you move through barriers which would normally stop you. Team building guarantees support as you strive to achieve outstanding results.

6. The sixth and final component of this process is CHOICE. In moving through change, you must always look for alternate ways to approach situations, other options, new possibilities.

How many ways can you move from point A to point B, with all of them being right? For example: Think of

**5**

10 ways to turn out a light... Did you come up with flick the switch? Break the light bulb? Turn off the circuit breaker or blow up the power plant? There is no right or wrong way to answer this question, since you are only examining a multitude of choices. Each choice leads you into new possibilities and different consequences.

And remember, even the smallest change in your life involves all six steps of the paradigm.

A note about the information that follows and the organization of this book.

Because your life and that of every reader is different, the pace and components of the change needed is likewise different. Change follows the six steps in the order suggested and presented; thus the book is organized that way. Yet the time and order at which you initiate change, and the number and variety of changes to be made by you and the many other readers preclude a step-by-step, do-this-then-that layout. So please read, evaluate, and apply the information, suggestions and observations as they serve your needs. The process that follows works if you do.

### THE MOMENT

*No anticipation*
*No expectation*
*And suddenly there appears*
*A gift*
*So wondrous*
*So simple*
*So beautiful*
*Brimming with tenderness, joy and hope*
*When one has faith, courage and fortitude.*

> Unless you are willing to be successful ...
> you cannot be successful.

## Understanding How to Look at Change

Now that you have an inkling of what the cycle of change is about, I want to warn you that it is a bit more complicated than it looks! No matter what the situation, you will never go through the six steps in perfect sequence, or alone. The steps appear in every imaginable combination and permutation—there is risk in awareness and trust in making choices.

To use a metaphor, you can put the six key concepts—Awareness, Willingness, Commitment, Risk, Trust, Choices around the clock—at 2:00, 4:00, 6:00, 8:00, 10:00 and 12:00.

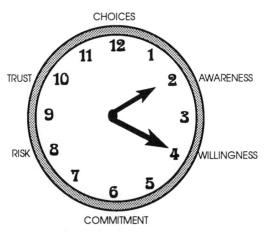

CHOICES

TRUST

AWARENESS

RISK

WILLINGNESS

COMMITMENT

Real time is seldom just 2 o'clock, but more often 2:10, or 2:47, or 2:16, so you can label 2:20 as being willing to become aware ('little hand' on awareness, 'big hand' on willingness); 4:30 as having a commitment to that willingness; and 2:30 as being committed to becoming aware!

Using examples and metaphors in various places throughout this book is important in giving you a basic sense of the changing process you go through, no matter how simple or how complex the change is.

This is a description of the normal steps everyone takes in making change. These steps are automatic and made on a subconscious level.

Remember—change is never easy; once started, it can sometimes be radical. Reading this book may be hazardous to your job, your relationships and your self-concept. As you change, you may find your job no longer fills your needs. Your relationships may not be conducive to your personal path of growth. You may find who you really are—deep down—is not who you have been trying so hard to be. (In my case, it meant a change in all areas of my life, career, family and self.)

Genuine change also implies growth. The purpose of this book is to help you grow toward a peace of mind which can only come with awareness, risk and change.

## COMPASSION FOR SELF

*The desire to listen carefully to one's own inner guidance.*
*The low energy, demanding attention in the realm of*
*quietness and silence.*
*To hear again the warbling, twittering, twirping of birds—*
*Meadowlarks, robins, wrens and jays.*

*The Peace that Passes Understanding.*
*Blending, harmonizing, synchronizing.*
*The music of the spheres fills my heart,*
*my spirit, my body.*
*The texture of the bark of the mighty redwood is craggy*
*and beautiful,*
*Just as my essence is both craggy and beautiful.*

*Life is what it is.*
*It is wondrous.*
*It is miraculous.*

# PART 1

# THE MOMENT—THE MOUNTAIN

## Chapter 1
### CLIMBING THE MOUNTAIN

## Chapter 2
### PAST, FUTURE, PRESENT

# CLIMBING THE MOUNTAIN

## The Mountain Called Life

*Who would have thought I'd ever contemplate climbing a mountain—certainly not me! Yet in 1989 I was given a brochure about a course in Neuro Linguistic Programming— a five-day work shop which involved mountain climbing. This had me flirting with the idea...*

*The mountain was Devil's Tower in Wyoming. Well, Devil's Tower was close to my home town and it did hold many fond memories for me. Yet I put the brochure aside, thinking it was silly to even consider it.*

*Just a week before the course, the flyer appeared again and it seemed to be calling me. I decided to consider my choice through visualization.*

*I imagined Devil's Tower in front of me. I asked myself, "How would I feel if I were there?" It was an adventure, exciting, exhilarating. I felt eager and a little bit apprehensive. I paid attention to my feelings. Then I shook out the visualization of the mountain and asked myself, "How would I feel if I stayed with my usual routine?" I felt resignation. It would be safe and secure perhaps, yet it was almost depressing.*

*It was clear to me what my preference was. Still I continued to argue with myself, saying I couldn't take the time off, it was too expensive and my family wouldn't approve.*

*(The fact of the matter is I have the time, energy, and money to do anything I want as long as I let myself. My family doesn't generally appreciate being the scapegoat for my indecision; rather, they truly support me in what ever it is I do. Only sometimes I don't want to believe it.)*

---

The past is where the drama is.

The present is where the action is.

The future is where the dreams lie.

Only the moment is real.

---

*Before the six steps of the paradigm are discussed, the mountain will be looked at as a metaphor for your life. Chapter 2 will examine your past, future and present and the affect of this on your life today. Chapter 3 is about who you are and who you want to be.*

## THE MOUNTAIN CALLED LIFE

This time I took the chance—I dared to join the NLP workshop and climb Devil's Tower.

The expedition proved to be a critical experience in my growth.

*I look up. There it is! Devil's Tower! It's rugged, it's beautiful.*

*I've joined a group of twenty other climbers at base camp. There are four master teachers who are leading this life event, each with his own area of expertise.*

*The weather is rainy and it is dusk. I wonder how camp is going to be set up in this mess! Scouts find a country store willing to shelter the team for the night. There are sleeping bags between aisles and under counters.*

*I'm asked by one of the leaders: "What do you have at stake in this climb?" I'm not sure. In fact I'm wondering why I am here at all.*

*With gentle probing I discover, or rather uncover, my willingness to live life in a different way. I want excellence with ease, power with passion and prosperity with play. I've had excellence, power and prosperity; but somehow the ease, passion and play were missing.*

*To me, this mountain represents the areas of my life I want to concentrate on: business and relationship. I am asked: "As you climb this mountain, what are your boundaries?"*

*I don't even know what is meant by boundaries!*

*It is explained that boundaries keep one within the limits of their personal integrity. Without boundaries, one would do anything, yes anything, to reach their life goals. Perhaps even cheating, lying, stealing or being covert.*

*I must answer these question authentically and from my heart. I have a very fine definition of integrity and I don't cut myself much slack. It is important for me to know just what my boundaries are and the limits of my integrity so I am able to live with myself.*

*The rain continues into the next day. I'm restless and ready to get on with it. I think about returning home but after having come this far I choose to stay. I begin to feel strange emotions in my body. Emotions like fear and panic! Tears fall and cleanse me just as the rain drops wash the dust from the leaves.*

*The next day, I am taken to some clay banks to learn about tracking and stalking animals. I don't know this is a part of the package and I wonder, "How does this affect my life?" Well, the way animals, even people, walk show what what it is that robs them of their energy. Imprints left upon the earth reveal energy*

**14**

levels and states of health and mind. One can determine whether the animal is wounded, scared, old, or controlled by time.

After learning what footprints can tell one about animals, I decide to study my own tracks. My footprints show time is my number one enemy. I don't walk on the earth gently but with the harshness of years of intentionality and purpose; of reaching my goals without weighing the costs.

Next, I am asked to be silent and to identify ten sounds of nature, sounds that are not man-made. The quiet is deafening. Eventually, my ears begin to adjust to the subtle sounds of the wind, falling leaves, and crickets.

I now have a new awareness of my surroundings. My senses have never been so acute. I am conscious of my finely tuned hearing, smelling, tasting, feeling, and seeing. I am now "present" to the mountain.

It is evening. The stars are as bright as I've ever seen. It's pleasant. There is excitement in the air, anticipation for whatever is next.

Time for some drumming and African dancing. I become mesmerized by the fire and the sounds of the drums. Everything is so foreign, yet I am not uncomfortable. I watch as my teammates, one by one, join in the movement and mystique of the moment. I can no longer be an observer and I too join in the circle of movement. My body takes over my mind and I move into a space and time previously foreign to me.

The next day the team is instructed on safety, how to use the ropes and the harness, how to belay, how to wedge finger holds. We practice climbing and repelling. I am surprised by how little time is spent on telling everyone to be awake and careful. I know how dangerous this can be if someone is not completely alert and aware. This team is inexperienced and the route chosen is difficult, even for experienced rock climbers. We take a day to practice climbing.

Suddenly the time is now! Equipped with all the paraphenalia, I am no longer even questioning my sanity. I am

**15**

committed to making this climb and don't doubt my ability to make it to the top.

It's my turn. The woman just before me doesn't make it. I watch as a male team member struggles with fear and returns to the bottom. The rope is snapped in place around me.

I start climbing. I move quickly, as if I've done this many times before. I am so "present" to the mountain. My options for finger and foot holds seem to jump out at me. My legs stretch and my arms seem to have an enormous amount of strength.

I hear my team mates rooting me on! I feel so light. I smile broadly. Then I come up against a wall of solid rock. I cannot see any crevices, any irregularities in the surface on which to step or to which I can grab hold.

I look frantically down at my buddy, who is holding my life rope in his hands. I shout, "There are no more places to go." Then, I am coached and guided to where I can again see my options. I look and move more slowly. I am seeing great barriers to reaching the top. But I am moving. Little by little and moment by moment, I climb. There is a ledge jutting out right before the top. I muster all my strength. I strain; I pull. With another giant shot of adrenalin, I'm THERE!

Excellence with Ease! Power with Passion! Prosperity with Play! I did it! I did it!

# Chapter 2

# PAST, FUTURE, PRESENT

*Break Out
Put the Past in Front of You
Climb into the Future
Be Present*

> When you watch a plant grow through a rock,
> you know that it was meant to happen.
> The seed has committed to life.

## BREAK OUT

To break out of the past, be aware of your purpose. Consider those things you think are missing in your life. Are they play, happiness, support, money?

The chances are, if you have enough money, you feel you don't have enough time—or energy. What then is the solution?

What is YOUR *mountain*? Does it exist? What does it look like? Is it covered with snow and ice? Does the rock crumble under your feet? Is there vegetation and wildlife?

What are the sounds of your *mountain*? How do you feel as you stand at the foot of your *mountain* and look to the top? Can you see the summit or is it shrouded in clouds?

Is there a path for you to follow? Or do you prefer to blaze your own trail?

Is this a solo journey or will you need ropes and a partner? Do you want a team to accompany you?

Is your physical body in shape for the climb? Are you calm or excited? How is your mental state? Emotional state? Spiritual state?

What is your vision? What do you stand for? Are you about raising a family? Caring for aging parents? Are you about peace and love? Are you about anger and resentment? Are you about making a difference in the world? Why are you on this planet we call the earth?

What would stop you from reaching the summit? What barriers have you created which will or could stop you from reaching the top? Do you have internal conversations like: "I've never made it to the top before, so why should it be different this time?" or "Every time I climb I get so beat up I don't know if it is worth it." Maybe you're hearing "I'm not good enough!" or "I can't!" or "Life is so hard!"

Most of us have little voices in our heads that sometimes have power over us. The trick is to be aware of the conversations you have with yourself, acknowledge that you are speaking both parts and then choose which *voice* you will act on.

What are your boundaries? To what lengths will you go to in order to reach the top?

You will want to consider the costs and benefits of reaching the zenith. There is a probability of the costs also being the very benefits you receive, as is discussed later in the book. The most important question for you to ask yourself is: "Is it really okay for my life to be okay?"

**18**

So you learn to balance your time, energy and money between your career, your relationships and yourself. You address the conflicts that arise. You tell the truth. You negotiate. And you listen to the small, still voice within.

The truth is—we aren't broken, we just keep waiting and hoping for some spouse, boss, book or motivational speaker to fix us!

### TRUTH

*What is it for me?*
*I know it is the beauty of the earth*
*I know it is the songs sung by birds*
*I know it is the fragrance of the flowers*
*It is the earth—damp, solid and immovable*
*It is the sky—with its limitlessness*
*It is life—with all the love, joy and sadness.*
*It is what is,*
*All that is,*
*All that isn't.*
*It is you*
*And it is me.*

---

Ease comes from the determination to break out
of self-imposed barriers.

---

# PUT THE PAST IN FRONT OF YOU

There is a towering mountain in front of you. You are here to climb, with ropes and all the other mountaineering gear. The mountain is steep.

**19**

You wonder what you are doing here and why you came. You have never climbed before. What is the purpose of this climb?

You ask yourself, "Do I want to climb? What if I don't make it? Am I willing to take the first step away from base camp? What are the risks and rewards of the climb? What do I have at stake in it? Am I willing to assure my leader we will win?"

If the answer to that question is "YES," then you are ready for the next step.

Once the decision has been made to change and you've committed yourself to the change, the next step in this process is ACTION. You start to do the preparatory work which will make way for the actual changes to occur.

Mentally you are beginning to FOCUS. (An example of focusing: Picture a funnel. It has one big, wide end and then tapers down to a small opening. Your thoughts are also being condensed and compressed, as if they are falling through the funnel.)

You may become irritated with the slightest distractions. Your body may begin to feel tension and you can't put your finger on what is going on.

You might want to snap at your colleagues and employees. Your family might be staying out of your way, thinking it's "one of those days." All it is, is your body getting ready for CHANGE.

Emotionally you may feel tired, scared, excited, energized. Mentally, you may wonder what on earth is happening. "Am I losing my mind?"

Yes, when you begin to make changes and take some risks, you may find yourself questioning your sanity. Change is not life *or* death, it is life *and* death. It's endings for new beginnings.

This is the time for you to look at your past. You have probably heard, "Put your past behind you." The only

**20**

trouble with this advice is it gives the impression of running from your past. Instead, put your past in front of you.

Imagine yourself high on a mountain. It's beautiful! There is lush green foliage with lots of pines, redwoods, rocks and wild flowers. You are looking down into a peaceful, sleepy valley.

This is a good place to put your past, right in this peaceful valley. From your vantage point on the mountain, you can see clearly, and for many miles. (Unless there is fog—and then you get to examine what that is all about!) There you can access any memory—either in your mind or in your body in order to see the gifts and lessons of the past. Your history becomes a source of learning, an awareness of who you have been. It lets you see patterns and make new choices based on your "education"—your past, called life. It is only when you stop running from the past that you will begin to benefit from it.

The goal or objective of this exercise is to glean any lesson, whether pleasant or not, the past has to offer. You want to be free from the fear of the same thing happening again. Paradoxically, it is this fear of repeating the past that will keep you in the rut of doing the same thing over and over again. It's like a hamster on a wheel, running with no place to go. Fear breeds fear, and more fear.

When you put the past in front of you, you can access it however you desire. You no longer have to run from it. You give up survival fears in return for faith and trust. Surrender to the universe and God.

**OPENNESS**

*The blackbird emerged,*
*Greeting and welcoming me to life.*
*He said, "I love you...*
*Breathe and let your body release, revitalize and reveal.*
*For you are an instrument of the one that is—*
*Do what there is to do.*
*Bringing love, laughter, life,*
*Filled with faith, freedom and frankness.*
*Be who it is you are—*
*All that it is you are—*
*And be not afraid.*
*There is nothing to fear."*
*The fog is lifting*
*And the truth shall be revealed.*

You can only live your own dream.

# CLIMB INTO THE FUTURE

As you climb the mountain, your future will not always be clear. There will be huge trees, boulders and small hills or valleys obscuring your view. Remember your first vision of the mountain. You stood back and viewed it with awe, seeing the total picture.

Your future is your vision. It will be built by the way you are currently designing your life. The path you are paving this moment is your future. If it is paved with judgements, blame and resentments, then that is exactly what your future will look like.

Each step you take today makes way for tomorrow. If you will be happy "when...", then you will be happy never; because that is when "when" is. All you have is this moment. Living in the future does not allow you to deal with the present. You climb into the future, one day at a time.

Take risks! Live this day as if it were your last. Then each day is complete and satisfactory without the "when's" and "if's."

## THE EYES OF RAIN

*When clouds shroud the mountain*
*And you can't see the peaks*
*You think life is dreary and cold.*

*You wait for the sun to shine*
*You wait for the mountains to expose themselves*
*You wait for your life to get better*
*You wait and wait and wait.*

*One day when you've had enough waiting—*
*You open your eyes*
*And see the mountains still there*
*Even with the rain, sleet, fog and clouds.*
*You see the gift each element,*
*Each condition brings.*

*And all of a sudden*
*You are aware the sun never quit shining,*
*And the mountain peaks are still there,*
*And life is grand and glorious*
*Just the way it is.*

> To take each moment,
> love each moment,
> live each moment.
> That's all there is!

## BE PRESENT

As you start your climb, be present to the hazards along the way. Be centered and grounded. Be totally aware of what is happening around you. There is no place for your mind to be, except present.

Let go of the past and the future if you wish to be in the present. How often have you sat over a delicious meal at a fine restaurant talking about another meal you had at a different place? Instead of enjoying the meal at hand, you are reliving a previous experience. Will this meal have to be talked about at a future time in order for it to be truly enjoyed?

It's just like the time I walked on the beach with a friend. He brought out some slides he had taken—of seagulls and the beach! The seagulls were right with us—yet mentally he was in a dark room with his slides and projector, not there enjoying *this time* at the beach.

When you hold on to negative past experiences, they fester and cause unease and later disease. When you push the present into the future, you lose it.

People are often like this with family and children. They may put off children's discoveries until "later" —until a more appropriate time. They tell them to "wait until..."

You may find yourself in the hospital with a dying friend or relative, bemoaning what "should have been done." Does it really matter what the past was or what the future is? Or is it important to just be with your loved one now, holding hands?

This is the time to give up the "should's" and the "have to's." This is the time to be present to the moment as you have never been before.

Accidents happen, *when you are not present to the moment*. When your head is not with you, you pass the exit on the freeway. When you are enjoying the rush of the air and the incredible beauty of the mountain slope and forget you are on skis, you crash.

When you are in the present, then you can be fully with your business, your loved ones, yourself.

### I AM

*I am a warrior, I am serenity.*
*I am the night, I am the day.*
*I am the sun at noon,*
*I am the moon at midnight.*
*I am the stars that twinkle and beam.*
*I am the wind caressing the trees.*
*I am the mountain.*
*I am.*

*PART 2*

# THE BEGINNING OF CHANGE

### Chapter 3
### LOOKING AT CHANGE

# LOOKING AT CHANGE

*Who Are You?*
*I'll Be Happy When*
*Breakdown for Breakthrough*

> The body, a microcosm for the macrocosm of our
> planet, the earth.

## WHO ARE YOU?

Have you ever asked yourself:

✤ Who am I?

✤ What do I want to do with my life?

✤ How do I want to be remembered?

✤ If this were the last six months of my life, what
would I want it to be like?

Big questions. And you must answer these questions
yourself. Your future is at stake.

It is possible be become so focused on the outcome of
projects that the important things in your day-to-day
living get put aside. Personal things (like your physical

health, exercise and diet), family needs (like hugs and time for quiet sharing), personal time (such as reading for the fun of reading or indulging in a hobby) are neglected.

Some successful business people are seemingly blessed with the ability to have tunnel vision. Nothing gets in the way of their target or expected outcome. But this same "blessing" is also the downfall of many. While they do whatever it takes to get the "work" done, their energy level leaves much to be desired when the "work" is completed. There is nothing left of who they are.

What was it that brought you joy as a child, as a teenager? Perhaps it was singing in the choir, dancing, playing basketball, reading science fiction, swimming or any of myriad other activities.

The question arises, what is this life all about? Some keep doing the same thing over and over again, like a hamster on a wheel. Some live life in the past or future instead of being in the now. They are always looking for joy, fun, enthusiasm—*tomorrow*. The past becomes the good old days. It's the "I will be happy when..." syndrome.

Do you sometimes wonder, "What am I doing with my life? Who am I?"

## I AM LIFE

*I am a rose. Gently unfolding and opening to the magnificence of the world.*

*I am light. Radiating God, so all who see me may experience joy and a renewed sense of purpose.*

*I am strong. Like a black panther, sleek and shiny with taut muscles, yet smooth and sensuous to the touch.*

*I am gentle. Like a new-born lamb, sweet-smelling and cuddly.*

*I am a singer. Others may find joy and comfort in words and melody.*

*I am beautiful. Pure white snow on a mountain top, inspiring.*

*I am trust. I trust my body to tell me—and I listen.*

*I am bright, intelligent. I create and make a difference.*

*I am cheerful. I sing the praises of God.*

*I am realistic. I know it takes action to make dreams reality.*

*I am action. I do what needs to be done. I do it joyfully and with love in my heart.*

*I am love—the purest and the finest.*

*I am life. Abundant and pregnant with new life to share.*

*I am guided by God's love and the Light of Christ.*

> Ask yourself,
> "Have I got it yet? Have I had enough?"
> For it is only when you've "got" the message
> that you have had enough.

## I'LL BE HAPPY WHEN ...

Do you look to the future and think:
- ☐ When I close that deal ...
- ☐ When my kids graduate ...
- ☐ When my divorce is final ...
- ☐ When I lose weight ...
- ☐ When I find a partner ...

Or perhaps you look at the past and remember when:
- ☐ There weren't all these job demands.
- ☐ The kids did as they were told without talking back.
- ☐ Life was simpler.

What, then, is your dilemma? Do you have it all? Perhaps you have a lovely home, a fine family, friends, expensive vacations and you're still saying: "I'll be happy when ..."

Perhaps you know someone who has material success in life and has achieved a life style envied by many. They worked hard to get where they are. They have lovely homes, cars and families. They are high-level employees or perhaps their spouses. They are committed, loyal and trustworthy. They work hard.

**31**

But it's not enough. Despite everything they have, they are not happy.

Perhaps this describes you. Do you think constantly about what you could do or should have done to make it better, to make it right?

Are you looking for direction—a way of life that puts you in touch with your purpose for being on this planet? Are you looking for other options, other ideas, other solutions?

You think, "It wouldn't take much to make me happy. If only my boss would realize how dedicated I am to this job. If only I could complete this one project. If only I could put in less than seventy hours per week. If only it were Saturday and I could rest. If only the kids didn't demand so much time, so much money."

And if only your employees or subordinates would get their personal lives in order (so they could work more efficiently). Or, if they could just get along better (so there would be less stress in the office). And if they would just finish that one project so you don't have to worry about it.

And your spouse would be perfect if he or she had these particular qualities, and got rid of those. For little did you know when you married this person their strengths were the same as their weaknesses. Those qualities that attracted you are the same ones you now find so undesirable.

For example, the child-like qualities of play and enthusiasm you fell in love with could be the same qualities you now label as irresponsible, tardy and thoughtless.

You look at your children. You wonder why they don't get better grades. Or you wish they wouldn't be so chunky, or that they didn't have so many friends. Or you wonder why they don't have any friends—whatever it is, it's not the way you would like it.

It is easy to forget that they, as well as you, are perfect for today. They are whole and complete for right now.

**32**

So this book isn't about getting somewhere. It isn't about being happy *when* … It's about being aware of who you are and where you are *now*. It's about deciding where you want to be, then deciding what changes to make in your business, your relationships, your life.

Be willing to give up the "reasons" you have for things not always being perfect. Be willing to try new things.

### TRANSFORMATION

*As the bear emerges from the cave*
*The butterfly from the safe secure cocoon*
*So I too emerge, as a standing bear*
*Awake, alert, hungry …*
*And with a purpose.*
*Just as the seasons come and go—*
*My power, my passion, my purpose*
*Become a sea*
*Sometimes quiet and serene*
*Sometimes stormy and turbulent.*
*However—always present to life, to love, to joy.*
*Always present to continuing change.*

> There are ghosts having to do with success
> in relationships and in business
> that terrorize us until there is no mobility.

# BREAKDOWN FOR BREAKTHROUGH

A phrase you will encounter frequently in this book is *Breakdown for Breakthrough*. *Breakthrough* is what this book is all about:

✣ Breaking through the old patterns of behavior that trap you in unhealthy relationships—in you business life as well as in your personal life.

✣ Breaking through the feelings of inadequacy and fear.

✣ Breaking through to a new happiness based on awareness, risk and choice.

In most projects, business endeavors and relationships, there is some degree of breakdown before breakthrough can happen. For example, your car flashes a warning light. You could choose to keep driving, but the consequences would be severe to the auto engine and to your wallet. Another choice is to stop the car.

People often run their lives in the same way, ignoring the warning signs until they are in complete breakdown.

*For many years I owned a real estate brokerage with my husband.*

*I had it all! I had a magnificent home, located in Northern California. It was like having Hawaii in my own back yard. Tall palms swayed gracefully near the pool that looked more like a*

**34**

*deep blue lagoon. There were towering redwoods, flowering fruit trees and rock gardens filled with fragrant flowers peeking out here and there.*

*I had a family, a spouse and two children—healthy and intelligent young fellows, very active, fun-loving, and full of spice and vinegar. My social life was full and I was active in and appreciated by the community.*

*It was fun going to the office, too! The agents and staff were always glad to see me. I used to stop and chat for a few minutes with each person. We seemed to have a mutual admiration society.*

*As a working broker, I was privileged to sell some of the most expensive homes in the area. Living in a big home and living life in the fast lane was a benefit. I could relate to the "big bucks" my buyers were spending.*

*I wasn't afraid to ask the buyer or seller any questions, since at heart I've always liked risk taking. I found the challenge of putting together a string of escrows fun and creative.*

*I also found joy in putting the first-time home owner into a property they never dreamed of owning. I watched their delight as they saw an ending to the insanity of rent and the beginning of equity.*

*Most of all, I enjoyed situations where I could use my creative abilities. I loved working with buyers who were willing "to find a way" to their dream and helping sellers to examine the benefits and costs of each offer.*

*Success, wealth and fantasy. Interesting combination. How clearly I remember the years of frantically trying to juggle the office management, my escrows, the buyer's and seller's needs and the needs of my family.*

*So what happened? You might call it burnout. I call it breakdown. I became so focused on getting to the destination that I forgot to enjoy the journey.*

*I had so closely structured my time that there was no time left for unexpected pleasantries. Even a "Thank You" card was put aside. Calls that said, "Thank you, you are special, I appreciate you," were not heard. To my spouse who said, "You are beautiful and talented" I replied, "Oh, thanks," but I never quite believed him.*

*Rarely did I have the time to watch my kids swim at a meet or listen to their dreams and fears.*

*I just kept going faster and faster on the merry-go-round of life until it didn't feel merry anymore.*

*When the merry-go-round stopped, I had to get off. The problem was, I no longer knew who I was, what I wanted or where I was to be. I had nothing more to give anyone, even me.*

*So the breakdown was the end of a 23 year co-dependent marriage, major surgery and treatment for alcoholism.*

*At the same time my youngest graduated from high school and my oldest from college.*

*I sold my half of the company and my home, then ran to a nearby community where I bought a house in need of remodeling. I proceeded to do extensive work on my house and my life.*

*The bottom, the breakdown, was truly a time to decide whether I wanted to live or die. I chose life—and decided to participate in it, full out!*

> There are many obstacles on the path.
> Many we see and on many we stumble.

*An acquaintance of mine, with her husband, invested in a restaurant where he was the chef. This restaurant provided top level service and first class food to a satisfied clientele.*

*This fine dining establishment was short of money—for expansion, for renovation, for equipment. This couple felt a cash investment, to be used for equipment, instead of shares as a salary bonus, would improve the kitchen. The chef could then perform the culinary miracles of which he was truly capable. (I'll be happy when ...!)*

*The investment led the owners to try for an expansion. The obliging chef, having just borrowed $10,000 to improve his own work space, agreed to take a reduced salary and a delay in kitchen renovations, in order to help the place to reach its full potential. (Everything will be perfect when ...!)*

*He was working a 70-hour week, taking in only enough money to meet the loan payments. However, the couple "hung in" for many months, because they knew that it would be better when ...*

*When the place went bankrupt a year later, the couple lost their investment as well as a year's hard work. The "when ..." became "if only—"*

+ *they hadn't expanded,*
+ *the money had been used as planned,*
+ *the owner had spent more time at the restaurant,*
+ *the owner's wife hadn't been so greedy.*

*If only, if only, if only!*

Take a look at the number of failed marriages in this country. Consider how many of these people remarry and have the same problems with the new spouse. Many just marry another name, another body and the same set of characteristics.

These people haven't understood the *breakdown*. They are happy to be rid of what they believe to be the problem: the other person, the circumstances, the marriage that didn't work. They don't see the real problem: an inability within themselves to break the old patterns.

When going through *breakdown*, there is a marvellous opportunity for choice. An opening for change is created, perhaps a breakthrough to a new level of self-awareness.

**37**

More and more single men and women are choosing to remain single until they receive the lessons and gifts from failed relationships. They are looking at letting go of old obsessions, replacing these with a commitment to live and love unconditionally.

These people may be attending workshops, spending time in nature, reading self-help books, joining support groups or perhaps even attending one of many 12-step programs. They have recognized the breakdown and are making changes in their lives.

*Breakdown* can be the opportunity for a breakthrough to finding happiness and contentment!

Now in Chapter 4, you can begin exploring the first of the six steps of the paradigm.

## *PART 3*

# THE INVITATION/AWARENESS

**Chapter 4**

**AWARENESS**

**Chapter 5**

**WILLINGNESS**

**Chapter 6**

**COMMITMENT**

# AWARENESS

*Enough is Enough*
*Patterns*
*The Insanity Cycle*
*Waking Up*
*Tiny Changes*
*Uncomfortable Situations*
*Stories*

> It is time for quiet.
> Time to go inside.
> Time to just see and to love
> the you that you find.

## ENOUGH IS ENOUGH

There may come a day when your life no longer works as it used to work. There may come a day when you've had enough—enough being tired going to the office, enough being tired coming home, enough going home to the family where it's not enough to be with them.

Many successful people don't know when ENOUGH IS ENOUGH.

You may not ever have been without. Possibly you cannot even relate to what it is truly like to be without. And yet, somehow, you still want more.

*To see me from the outside, one might say I had it all. And many of us do "have it all", but just take a look at what we use in our daily lives to medicate, to numb the pain of the "not enough" syndrome.*

*I looked in my closet. I had enough clothes to share with several women! I looked in my pantry. There was enough food to feed a large gathering!*

*I took a look at how many friends I had calling me. How many friends I NEEDED, so I would have calls to return. I needed to be needed. To share their pain and joy was another way of medicating my own pain.*

*A glass of wine after work helped to soothe many things. It was a time to celebrate the success I had had in the business world, the big transaction I had cleverly put together. It was a time when I could relax with my partner, my company and my friends, without having to look at uncomfortable emotional issues.*

*One thing I knew, I was not going to come from scarcity! I was going to make sure that I and those around me had enough. It would happen if only they would do what I wanted them to do ..., if only they would TRY harder ..., if only they were more committed ..., if only ..., if only ...,*

*The only problem was that I didn't realize that I didn't have the power to control my own life, let alone others people's lives.*

*What was my bottom? It was losing everything in my life I loved the most.*

*My children were grown. My spouse was no longer committed to our marriage. I loved the family I had married into—and it was time to let them go. I loved the community I lived in, yet I moved.*

*I had plenty of friends and family. What I didn't have was a relationship with myself!*

**41**

*I didn't know what I liked, or what I wanted to do. I didn't know how to entertain myself without pleasing others.*

*As I said earlier, my bottom was a year filled with a broken marriage, selling property, moving, remodeling, workshops, seminars, treatment for alcohol addiction, major surgery and learning to take care of myself at the age of forty-three.*

*I had been so "taken care of" that I had never washed a car, mowed a lawn or cleaned gutters. These were a few of the things I was to learn about!*

*My bottom was filled with tears, broken dreams and an incredible desire to live. I just kept taking one tiny step at a time. I just kept on moving, because if I had stopped and fallen, I don't know if I could have gotten back up.*

*Others loved me until I could learn to love myself.*

---

I clearly see my addictive nature.
The rush that comes from trying to get my way;
from trying to get it all done now.

---

It happens sometimes—you raise your children, keep a lovely home, entertain lavishly, manage the office, motivate employees—you are always there for others, even if it seems no one is there for you.

Then comes *breakdown*; a total destruction and transformation of being. A descent into an unknown land on a path filled with risk, adventure and excitement.

Scraping bottom, my choice was to live or die. The moment I committed to live fully day by day, minute by minute, miracles began to occur. My life changed.

**42**

### EARTHQUAKE

*Everything around you moves—*
*You hold on for dear life*
*Like a merry-go-round*
*Moving faster, faster*
*Until you can move no more.*
*It becomes survival—*
*Moment by moment.*
*Lay flat*
*Where the least amount of damage can occur.*
*How can you survive until it's over?*
*This too shall pass.*

---

An observer changes what is occurring.

If you can see the path, the path changes.

Remembering that you remembered it, changes it.

---

# PATTERNS

What is happening when you feel strong emotions? Feelings of frustration, anger, sadness, joy, love, happiness? Where are they coming from?

Are you aware of patterns of behavior in your life? What are these patterns? When did they start? Why are they useful? How can you let go of old patterns which may keep you locked in dysfunctional behaviors? Becoming aware of your patterns and habits allows you to change them, allows you to be at choice.

Go back in your life. Consider the things that made you feel either good or bad.

* What activities were they?

* What were you doing?

* What did you look like?

**43**

✤ Who was with you?

✤ What did you feel?

✤ What did you think?

Your senses—touch, taste, sight, hearing, smell—are the way you receive information. As you have a sensation, the mind relates it to past experiences using your full range of memory; not just thought memory, but the deeper memory that lies within the body itself.

Next the mind gives an evaluation: the sensation is pleasant, or it is unpleasant. Finally the mind reacts. You like or dislike something because you like or dislike your reaction to the sensation.

Too often it is easier to cling to the things you like and avoid the things you dislike, sometimes obsessively. When you do, you are caught in patterns and lose your balance.

## PATTERNS

*Change is occurring;*
*I'm choosing it.*
*Letting go of old*
*To make room for new.*

*It's hard letting go of friendships—*
*They're like a comfortable slipper.*
*But they keep me stuck*
*In patterns, expectations, perceptions.*

*If I choose to move forward*
*On my path,*
*Then letting go with love*
*Is the perfect thing to do.*

*I am not wrong,*
*They are not wrong.*
*Each of us is exactly where*
*We should be.*
*Growing, stretching, yearning, learning.*
*On our own perfect path.*

> You have a choice.
> When you've been around
> the insanity cycle once,
> you can decide if you've had enough...
> or if you need
> to go around it one more time...
> or maybe five more times.
> The choice is yours.

## THE INSANITY CYCLE

Have you ever gone to work saying, "Today will be different?"

✦ I'll sell my quota today.

✦ I'll handle the problem with the supervisor.

✦ I'll discuss that issue with the General Manager.

✦ Today is the day I'll complete this project.

But when the time comes, you don't discuss the issue or handle the problem because you're afraid. You don't sell your quota or complete the project because of a fear of failure, or fear of success. You procrastinate until there just is no time left in the day to reach completion. Fear stops you from breaking the old pattern.

Part of the problem may be that you are not willing to do whatever it takes to let today be different. You might allow yourself excuses—the phone wouldn't quit ringing, the GM was too busy, I couldn't make an appointment, I simply ran out of time. You may be acting as if you are not in control of your choices.

**45**

In order for *life to be different* from what it has been, you have to *do something different*. You have to take a step in another direction, be creative, be willing to be ridiculed, rejected, or heaven forbid, reprimanded. You have to be willing to take a risk and experience failure.

To be alive means to have a purpose. Each person's purpose is individual and unique. Each person is on a journey. Many don't know where it's taking them, but they just keep putting one foot in front of the other.

Most people are either walking the *breakdown-for-breakthrough* path or the Insanity Cycle.

Rita Mae Brown defines insanity as doing the same thing over and over again expecting different results.

When you are in the Insanity Cycle, you might feel blissful, joyful, happy, angry, sad. Eventually, however, life as you know it no longer works. You feel confused. You become anxious, perhaps ashamed. If forced to make a decision, you might become angry or fearful. If you avoid making a decision, you feel inadequate as if you can do nothing right.

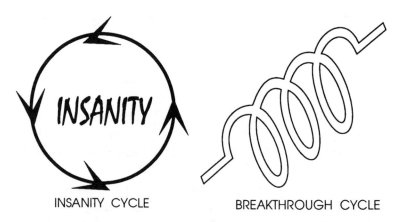

INSANITY CYCLE                    BREAKTHROUGH CYCLE

It may be that you can accept neither change nor the status quo. It seems easier to stay where you are, but you know something is wrong. You are stuck in denial, avoiding decisions and action, repeating old behaviors... and hoping this time the result will be to your liking.

You may not want to admit to "not knowing." It is somewhat unnerving to discover you do not have a clear picture of what's going to happen next. This is when panic sets in. You may get into a tailspin and frantically begin to search through the computer system, called the brain, in a futile attempt to understand the situation and control it.

*I remember so clearly the period of time when I sat down to write out what I wanted my life to look like. I looked at all my options. I began to question every option I had, from career objectives to a relationship with a life partner.*

*What did I want? How did my body feel when I mentally removed it from the safety and security of my present home and relocated it to a point in Southern California? How did my body feel when I imagined living in a rural area of Northern California without many of the conveniences and privileges I now experience? How would I feel if I moved to British Columbia where there was plenty of clean air, beauty, water and mountains, yet lots of rain and foggy days?*

*I knew that where I moved would impact my career, relationships and business. Each location would bring about new changes, challenges and confusions. I asked again, "What do I want? What feels good?"*

*I didn't know the answers so I decided to be with my indecision and let it clear in its own time. Now was my turn to enjoy the journey to my future. I had often heard, "Patience is a virtue".*

**47**

## PATIENCE

*Patience means not on my time schedule, but thine.*
*Patience means being fully present each moment,*
*living for this hour, minute.*
*Patience means petting my cat,*
*doing the dishes,*
*waiting for a red light to turn green—*
*and not being resentful.*
*Patience is eating a green salad*
*when you have braces!*
*Patience is talking to your own mother or your children.*
*Patience is—waiting for the right answer.*

---

When you are at a point in your life
where everything feels confused,
relax and enjoy the moments,
the hours and the days of confusion.

---

You may try to blame others for your problems, gathering evidence for how you have been victimized. In the process you become the prosecutor of the person you feel has victimized you. You fail to notice the sign hanging around your own neck, reading: EASY PREY!

*One of my clients is a teacher. She teaches in a school district that includes in its contract the right to professional autonomy in the classroom.*

*This teacher is recognized as an expert in her field. Unfortunately, she has not always had a strong belief in herself.*

**48**

*She became the target of harassment by a new principal. Hurt by the criticism, she felt not good enough, unacknowledged, belittled. There was a margin of truth in the criticism, but she felt she had to defend herself. By gathering twenty pages of evidence and by complaining to others she gained support for her side.*

*Saying, "I don't have to put up with this!" she took him to a grievance committee and won. For a time she felt superior, but she soon realized she had not really "won" after all.*

*However, the real problem had been masked. She had not been open to hearing the principal's concerns and problems; and ignored the correct criteria for judgement, she opened herself to abuse.*

The problems is, you can only be what your own self-image and belief system tells you that you are.

| IF: | THEN: |
|---|---|
| You believe your ideas are going to be rejected by your superiors... | ...they probably will be. |
| You are afraid of being disliked for stating your position in a relationship... | ...you set yourself up for failure. |
| You feel that whatever you do isn't good enough... | ...it won't be. |

You may be afraid the problem will happen again and again. And it does because you have not changed your basic premise.

You may be withholding permission from yourself to do what it is you really want to do. You make up excuses,

**49**

you blame other people, you even make up stories about how others might perceive you. Yet it is all related to how you perceive yourself.

Once you are aware of this process, you can become committed to breaking the endless cycle. Then you will be ready to risk and try out, to take steps that will lead you through Breakdown to Breakthrough.

> The first step towards living life fully
> is to realize you are asleep.

# WAKING UP

Awareness is waking up to what is going on inside yourself and around yourself. It is simply noticing how things are. It is just like when the spring rains come. One day you become aware of the new bright green growth, when just yesterday you didn't see it.

How do you know you are asleep? How do you wake up and see how to move through your life? As long as things are working for you, it is natural just to accept things as they are. But you are not aware of what's really going on. It's only when things don't work any more that you are apt to be willing to look at the truth and at options for change.

### *INTENTION*

A distinction between being asleep and being awake: Driving down the freeway with the blinker on while the intention is to go straight. Or being so involved singing along with the radio that you fail to notice the cop beside you, motioning for you to pull over. The intention has not been to speed, yet there you are merrily speeding down the freeway in the fast lane.

If you are asleep, you forget to look at the present—at what's going on right now, at what is squarely in front of your eyes. You are caught in the past/future view of things. "It has always looked like this and it will always look like this. It's always going to be the same because that's the way it is".

It often takes a major incident, a crisis, a breakdown—intentional or unintentional—to finally become aware of the implications and the options for change. The problem is, we don't know what we don't know. And, on the other side of the coin, we often don't know what we do know.

What can you do to become aware of what it is that's keeping us in our fantasy world and preventing us from moving into reality? What are the warning signs?

First, perhaps, there is no joy—in the workplace, in the home, in relationships or in our lives. Maybe little things are not being handled. Sometimes integrity, honesty and service are missing.

### HONESTY

When people want what they want, they will use all sorts of covert means to get it. They please, they pamper, they serve. Most often this also comes with a huge expense. When the victim of the control decides that their boundaries have been violated, the issue of trust is raised. Why don't people just ask for what they want? To be able to say: "I want to have dinner with you, do business with you, work with you, tell you how I'm feeling." Then the relationship can be one of honesty, with all concerned being honored.

Maybe your staff is running on auto-pilot, not hearing what is being said. Perhaps your family is reacting rather than responding. Perhaps you yourself formulate answers when you haven't even heard the question. Maybe there is not enough time, too much time. Maybe...

Sometimes a small incident, a minor deviation from the norm, can be the spark which suddenly opens your eyes. It can be similar to the tiny changes that are made by braces on your teeth, or the sudden realization that hunt and peck typing has become touch typing.

*Until I had a baby, I had no idea what it was like to deliver. Until I experienced each stage of their lives with them, I had no idea of the gladness and sadness to come from watching these little ones evolve into young adults. Until my kids went to college, I had no idea how freeing, yet lonely, it would be for them to leave home.*

*Until I quit smoking, I had no idea what it was like to breath clean air into my lungs.*

It doesn't have to be a lightning bolt. It may be a gentle nudge that does it. All of a sudden there's a shift. Awareness happens and you can't know it until it does.

You may be playing a game of tennis and suddenly, after umpteen lessons and even more practice, you have a sense of the fast or slow ball and you know how to react. You listen to your body and you just know. If you listen to your mind, you get confused. While you're trying to decide whether it's a high ball or a low ball, a backhand stroke or a forehand stroke, it's gone and your opponent has scored.

There's a sense of, "I don't know why this is the right thing to do, I only know it is." We visualize how it will be and let it happen. The awareness is in the body, at a very deep level.

Being awake involves accessing the unconscious. Being awake involves knowing where we spend our time, energy and money. This is not just time and energy spent at the office, but also being awake to and aware of how we spend our time on the twenty-four hour clock. As we start to look at life head on, it can become painful and we can easily fall asleep again.

### SAFETY

*Stay awake
Don't fall asleep!
It only takes one second
One flick of the eye,
It happens as quickly
As a falling star—
Never again to be.*

*The path gets narrower
And narrower.
Choices become fewer and fewer.
Once I see clearly the way to be—
Never again is the old acceptable—
Or an option.*

*Safety—yes!
Stay awake—
Accidents are a result of falling asleep.
They are a wake-up call to life
And the gifts of life.
Be joyous
Be receptive
Be thankful
For life and life's lessons are but gifts—
Precious, intangible, irreplaceable.*

> With dreams come challenges.
> Risky challenges!
> Sometimes so risky
> it seems impossible
> that one should ever succeed.

## TINY CHANGES

I keep remembering, THIS TOO SHALL PASS. And it always does.

*Part of my dream included presenting myself in what I perceived to be the best possible light. Therefore I decided to put braces on my teeth. Quite a project for a person whose children were in braces many years prior!*

*Then came scheduling visits to the orthodontist, watching the huge shifts and enduring the discomfort and inconveniences that come from making any change. In a way this process was a metaphor for my life.*

*When I learned it was time for my braces to come off, I felt panic! I was not only wondering if my teeth would remain stable long enough for the retainer to be made, but more importantly, the big question, "Was I ready for my life to be in order?"*

*As Richard Bach eloquently writes in his book ONE, "A tiny change today makes for a dramatically different tomorrow." All the tiny changes I have gone through every day—some seemingly of little importance, some major and some I was barely aware of—all evolved into Today.*

> My loneliness is the result
> of me not being there for me.

## UNCOMFORTABLE SITUATIONS

Many of us seem to be missing a purpose in our lives. You may come across a situation where you feel uncomfortable. It could be a board meeting, a sales meeting, a family gathering or a meeting with a friend. If it doesn't appear to be working for you, ask yourself:

- What is going on here?
- What is trying to happen?
- What is missing?
- What is my objective in being here?

Take a look to see if you are up against one of your personal barriers. Is this the best use of your time, energy and money? If this were the last day of your life, would you be here—in this place, doing this activity? What are the costs and benefits of this situation?

After a while it takes no time at all for you to know what is appropriate for you, your family or your organization. Most important, pay attention to your body. What is your physical reaction to the situation? When you look inside you know what to do.

NASA officials decided to use a cat in their space-sickness studies during the early days of astronaut training. One of the devices simulates the weightless conditions of outer space. It is a chair that can move side to side, up and down, and back and forth all at once.

Because cats have physiological similarities to humans, scientists decided to put a cat in the chair and observe its reactions. The first experiment was a success. They strapped the cat in, turned the chair on and studied the cat until it got sick.

The cat was a fast learner. The next time the cat saw the chair it immediately became ill.

The scientists were both amazed and amused. The cat responded to the entire situation, not merely to the effects of the experiment itself.

Like the cat, do you leave situations which you know are going to be uncomfortable or possibly even harmful? Or do you go through the discomfort because you feel you ought to?

---

There are two kinds of stories.
One is an elaboration
of a fairly simple event
or piece of information, ad infinitum.

The second kind
is a fabrication
designed to allow us to escape
or excuse ourselves for something.

---

## STORIES

Both kinds of stories work to take up time, to fill up space. A commitment to change means giving up the stories and probably giving up listening to them as well.

Stories can be wonderful. They can be playful, light, scary or heavy. One can evoke all sorts of emotions with them. Stories can be very dramatic and they can easily pull your listener in. The listener gets transported to the place and time of the story.

The feelings of the storyteller get transferred to the listener and a good storyteller has complete control over the audience. While this may be wonderful in an audience setting, it can be disastrous in relationships.

Stories can be helpful when used to access our memory bank for learning about our choices. We can instantly remember how we reacted, responded and felt at any one time. We can then decide on our options for action. However, when we remain stuck in the past we are not present to what is happening now, this very moment, this very day.

The biggest cost of listening to stories is in the expenditure of time and energy. Ask yourself, "Is this something I need to know, or is this something the speaker needs to say? Do I want to hear this, or is the speaker demanding I listen?"

Relationships in our society, both on the corporate level and the personal level, have become so entangled with stories that it is difficult for us to distinguish between fact and fiction. We embellish the facts and make the point hard to hear. Consequently, communication is scrambled.

We write scripts, both ours and theirs, before we even start a conversation with another person. We get so emotionally involved with the drama we often don't see the problem. You've heard the old cliche, "He couldn't see the forest for the trees."

If you over-embellish, exaggerate or excessively dramatize your stories in order to make a point, you may very well lose the listener along the way.

Inane chatter and conversations (where the same thing is said over and over, where nothing different is presented, where your comments have no point and do not communicate a message) are as dysfunctional and time wasting as stories that veer too far from reality.

People want to hear the bottom line, the facts, in order to make logical decisions. What stories can hide from our view is the truth.

Try to answer each of the following questions in one sentence:

- What is the problem with my organization?
- What is the problem with my significant other?
- What is the problem with my relationship with my children?
- What is the problem with my relationship with my parents, brothers, sisters, co-workers, employees, manager?

As you attempt to answer these questions, just notice the stories coming up. Be aware of your feelings. Be conscious of the enmeshment—the blame, the self-victimization, your martyr role.

Or, you may be saying, "there's nothing wrong with any of my relationships." In that case, just be grateful!

As you look at your answers (the version of the problem without story) you may begin to find some common elements. Are people angry? Unsympathetic? Complainers? Are they kind? Supportive? Gentle?

Whatever it is you see in them—may be who you are.

> Others are mirrors for us
> to see who we are.

When you...
- eliminate the story, theirs and yours,
- stop planning, "what if... ,"
- stop hearing, "if only I had... ,"

**58**

then you're left with what is. You're able to be aware of and to acknowledge your feelings and your inner understanding of what does and doesn't work for you.

Giving up the story means taking a risk. If we get to the bottom line, we may have to deal with it. We may have to know what's going on and cut out excuses.

### RISKING FRIENDSHIP

*Please be up front with me. I look for the good in all people. I don't expect the worst.*

*Tell me your intentions, so that I need not become suspicious of what it is you ask.*

*Listen to what I say. Sometimes it's as if we never discussed an issue... yet I know I have been clear. I know I have been heard. When you ask a question, don't ignore my answer.*

*I protect myself. I become suspicious. I will not play this game. The party's over. Too bad... it could have been wonderful.*

# Chapter 5

# WILLINGNESS

―――――――――――――――――――――――――――――

*The Authentic Yes*
*Willingness*
*Barriers*

---

> When we listen, the answer is there.
> Quiet your mind
> so you can hear what is being said.

---

*Willingness is the second step in the paradigm for change.*

## THE AUTHENTIC *YES*

*When I decided to write this book, I retreated to British Columbia for a month. I had been wanting a new car as my previous car no longer fit my image.*

*What I had to do in order to purchase a new car involved more than a little bit of risk taking. I looked at what was at stake.*

*I looked at it as if this were the last six months of my life. Would I buy a car so I could feel free and unlimited and creative as I journeyed 1000 miles to another country? Did I have myself covered in case of the worst scenario? When I weighed out the costs and benefits, was I willing to take the risk?*

*I talked to friends and personal coaches, my CPA, my financial planner, my oldest son. I listened and heard what they said.*

*Then I made my own decision.*

*I bought a brand new burgundy convertible. Whew! It is beautiful! And what a joy it is to drive! Did I make the right decision? The answer is an authentic YES!!*

*I focused on the risk. I focused on the mountain. Yes, at times I questioned my sanity. And it didn't stop me.*

And it was okay. The purpose of coaches is to bring to our attention obstacles and challenges we are not already seeing. They are not there to make decisions for us, but rather to be impartial observers.

You see, any decision is the right decision as long as we weigh out the cost and benefits and are willing to accept the worst. The worst will most likely not happen. But if it does, we can improve on it by going through the process: awareness, willingness and commitment.

A key step is to ask yourself these two questions, one at a time, and see if you can answer them with an authentic YES or NO.

☐ Are you willing to have work, life, relationships be different than they have been in the past?

☐ Are you willing to have work, life, relationships be different than what you think they SHOULD look like in the future?

Any answer other than a clear YES, is a NO. In other words, if you start on a story, (if...; maybe...; if only...; perhaps...) then it is not clearly "YES" and your answer is "NO." Accept that as your truth.

## PLAYTIME

*Playtime is...*
*Sharing intimate secrets with a special friend.*
*Touching a child's soul through an eye connection.*
*Experiencing the joy of seeing the world through the eyes*
*of a child.*
*Walking and talking.*
*Caring and sharing.*
*Splashing and thrashing.*
*Dancing with your adult child.*
*Running on the beach.*
*Driving a convertible.*
*Joyfully meeting new friends*
*And letting them see who you are.*
*Sitting in a hot tub*
*Alone*
*Or with someone.*
*Sitting beneath the stars and the moon.*

---

A real willingness—
to look at your company life, your family life,
your relationships, yourself—takes courage.

---

# WILLINGNESS

Carefully weigh out the costs and benefits of change. Then there can be balance, stability and forward movement. From this will come a realization of how to finely tune your company, your job, your relationships, your life, so they are moving forward with ease.

## EXPECT WHAT YOU EXPECT

*If you expect and give love,*
*you will receive love.*
*If you expect to be seen,*
*and you see all others, you will be seen.*
*If you expect to be heard,*
*hear others first,*
*and they will hear you.*
*If you expect to get things accomplished,*
*you will—if you apply action.*
*Only our own perception of what is,*
*is so for us.*

Look at your willingness to have things be different.

☐ Are you willing to take an in-depth look at your career?

☐ Are you willing to look at your relationships with those around you ?

☐ Are you willing to look at how you live your life?

Look at your willingness to see how happy the people in your life are—how often they smile or frown—when they cry or laugh—if they play and fight—whether they enjoy life or merely survive.

Examine your willingness to listen to your own body, to see what it is telling you about the way you treat it, what you feed it, how well you exercise it, how fit it is to carry you through your life.

Willingness brings freedom of choice. We have the choice to feel good or not good, be in reality or in fantasy, create action or create lethargy, be open to possibilities or be into excuses.

## OBEDIENCE

*I don't like to be obedient!*
*The word makes me bristle,*
*It makes me want to turn*
*And go in the other direction.*
*Then I remember—*

*What I resist persists.*
*And I look at what it means to me*
*To be obedient.*
*In old learning habits,*
*It means doing what another*
*Says is right for me to do.*

*Now I know—*
*If it is not right for me,*
*It is certainly not right for you.*

*It means having the courage to tell the truth,*
*It means courage to travel a path*
*That is uniquely mine,*
*And let you have your path*
*Which is uniquely yours.*

---

What I was not prepared for
was my own self-imposed barrier.

---

# BARRIERS

*When I think about willingness I think about whether I want to do something or not. And sometimes I don't know. As I work on a project, I find my eyes growing heavy. I want to go to sleep. I am not tired—just up against my own personal barrier. This barrier comes in the form of completion.*

*I ask myself, "What is going on here?" I am on my home stretch and I must again ask myself: "Is it okay for me to be*

**64**

*successful? Is it okay for me to complete a huge project and not to know what lies ahead for me? Is it okay for my life to be okay?"*

In all sports, timing is critical. This sense of timing becomes a part of body awareness. When you learn a sport, you concentrate on the specifics. As you practice and learn, your muscles are developing a memory.

Even as you model someone else, following their instructions, it is all trial and error for your own body. In the final analysis, our learning comes from doing—a point is reached when you just do it, without thought.

Sometimes a golf shot isn't good, or you can't seem to put a spin on the backhand stroke when playing tennis. If you analyze each step as you perform the action, you can become hopelessly bogged down.

If you wish to change and improve and if you wish to push through your barriers, ask an expert to observe your actions and assess the relative merits of each move. Then change one thing at a time.

In sports, you can usually accept that someone is better than you are and accept help and support. Suggestions for change are not taken personally. You know with practice, you can change the way your muscles react to stimuli. Barriers are recognized as training opportunities.

In a career/working situation it is easy to become more protective of the way you do things. In other words, competition in sports is seen as a challenge to physical ability. Competition on the job is seen as a threat to your thoughts, to your very identity. You may put up what you think of as protective barriers, but they can hinder you from learning and moving forward

It must be realized that work behavior is based on action the same as sports behavior—as learned body responses.

Whether your response to a situation is muscular, verbal or emotional, it is a learned and conditioned response. Your reaction to a criticism in the workplace is as automatic as the golf swing that slices a drive into the woods. Both can be changed, with awareness, instruction and practice.

Not every new situation creates a barrier. You may be constantly learning, changing, adjusting and reviewing the way you do things. Many things you come up against can be easily overcome by applying old understandings to new situations. It is when you come up against a barrier which can't be move through quite so easily, that you are stumped. You may try everything, but nothing seems to work.

Become aware of the little things that hold you back. Examine your body response to different situations and if necessary, allow an outside observer to show you where to make adjustments.

## LISTENING

*How does it feel to truly listen to your body? To hear its subtle messages? First, there are feelings of discomfort and unease. Your mind says, "Maybe this is another barrier to push through, or maybe it's now okay for me to be where I'm meant to be."*

The truth is that there are no barriers you cannot remove from your lives. In order to accomplish this, you have to think of the procedures used to eliminate the small, everyday barriers and apply this process to the "insurmountable" ones.

## STEPS TO GO THROUGH THE WALL

1. You encounter a barrier.

2. You don't like it and wish it would go away.

3. It persists and becomes more dense.

4. You throw a tantrum.

**66**

5. You kick it and scream at it.

6. It's still there. You can climb over, crawl under, go around or go through.

7. You soften to the pain and stop the suffering.

8. Then you clearly see your choices.

9. You go play.

10. When it doesn't leave you alone and you've had enough, you surrender with ease.

11. Suddenly you notice you're on the other side.

12. You celebrate your success.


### SUCCESS

*I did it! I did it!*
*It feels grand!*
*I bridged a gap*
*And with this new expanse comes*
*new opportunities*
*new vistas*
*new horizons*
*Hoorah!*

# Chapter 6

# COMMITMENT

*Commitment versus Obligation*
*Commitment versus Obsession*
*A Sense of Purpose*
*Happiness*

---

> We can't do anything without intention.
> When we intend, it is just so.

---

*The third step of the paradigm is commitment.*

## COMMITMENT VERSUS OBLIGATION

*I used to commit myself easily. These days, I have difficulty making commitments. What I feel, want, desire today is not necessarily so for me tomorrow.*

*I weigh business decisions carefully and relationship commitments also. I dislike breaking commitments to others —it's easier to hang loose.*

*When I commit fully to a project, miracles do occur. There is the time, the energy and the money for it to happen. And it does.*

Thoreau so beautifully said it all:

"I learned this at least by my experiment—that if one advances in the direction of his dreams and endeavors to live the life which he has imagined, he will meet with a success unexpected in common hours. He will put some things behind, will pass an invisible boundary: new, universal and more liberal laws will begin to establish themselves around and within him: or the old laws be expanded and interpreted in his favor in a more liberal sense, and he will live with the licence of a higher order of being."

> Remember always that you have a choice.
> Even after you commit,
> you can choose to change your mind.
> The only cost of this
> is owning up to a mind change.

Commitments are not obligations. A commitment is an agreement to do something now or in the future, on a pledge or promise. An obligation is a moral or legally binding course of action.

It can be very difficult getting out of commitments when they no longer work—when the costs outweigh the benefits.

Too often the easiest way to break a commitment is to lie, make up stories or make excuses.

❖ I couldn't because…,

❖ I would have except…,

❖ I couldn't get that out in the mail today because…,

❖ I would have done it, but I didn't understand…,

**69**

The question is, how can you design your life to make it work? Getting out of commitments when they no longer work for you is vital. And that may be a one-shot commitment like a dinner engagement. It might be a short-term commitment, such as committee work for an upcoming conference. It might be a long-term commitment to an employee or employer. It might be what some consider a life-time commitment—marriage.

If it no longer works for you, for whatever reason, tell the truth without the stories.

### POWER IS BEING ABLE TO...

*...be at ease, to center, to calm.*
*...respond rather than react.*
*...keep life simple, uncomplicated.*
*...be with what is occurring.*
*...stay in the present—*
*...stop projecting into future days, hours, moments.*
*...say, "Thanks for asking" and "It doesn't work for me".*
*...have the presence of mind to listen to my body, hearing when it's crying for relief from the constant motion, I keep it in.*
*...handle whatever is in front of me, always present to my power of choice and my capacity to make decisions.*
*...take time to listen to the melody of the birds, observe the beauty of a rose along the path.*
*...smell the aroma of freshly baked bread and the poignant scent of evergreens.*
*...look into the eyes of a child and see the beauty and innocence therein*
*...tell the truth to yourself.*

When you are aware of your behavior and your feelings, you can acknowledge them and accept them as part of who and what you are. You can choose to continue a commitment or not, and you can do it without making yourself or others wrong!

### FOUNDATION

*The foundation the mountain rested on*
*Dissipates like a rising fog*
*Unveiling a slender, flexible bamboo shoot*
*A pillar of strength,*
*Flexing in the breeze and wind.*

> I pray, surrender, cry, pout,
> and start the cycle all over again!

# COMMITMENT VERSUS OBSESSION

As well as making commitments to others, we make commitments to ourselves—to growth and change. There is a fine line, however, between commitment and obsession. An obsession is an excessive, persistent, disturbing preoccupation with a thought or feeling.

You may be committed to getting your golf handicap down. To do so you practice and play regularly. Or you may become obsessed by the game—giving excess time, energy and money to improving your game, to the exclusion of all other goals. The obsession takes over your life. If only you had just a little more time, a little more energy.

I have a friend who sometimes finds herself working on the computer into the wee hours of the morning. She knows rest is needed to be functional the next day, but she occasionally spends too much time on the computer before fully acknowledging her tiredness, therefore losing needed energy she will regret.

She is aware of this obsessive behavior. She has examined the costs. At this time she accepts the consequences without berating herself. When she does become willing to

**71**

change, then she will make a commitment and will experience a greater degree of success.

For life and life's lessons are gifts—precious, intangible, irreplaceable. If you don't learn the lesson the first time, you will be privileged to do it over and over and over again, until you do get it.

I ask myself, "Do I have it yet? Have I had enough?" For it is only when I've got the message that I have had enough.

### RUNNING

*How Fast I Run*
    *Moving Always*
    *Don't stop!*
            *Those feelings will show!*
    *Keep moving!*
            *Faster, faster, faster.*

*I feel like a brick,*
    *just made... .*
    *tight,*
    *solid,*
    *rough edges,*
    *colored that reddish clay color...*
            *The brick has a lot of holes...*
    *And — if you drop me—*
    *I will break*
    *into unusable, ineffective pieces.*

*When will I stop*
    *long enough for me to hear—*
    *for me to receive*
    *the love of my universe,*
    *the love of humans—*
    *the love of life?*

> A Recipe For Life:
> Love, love and love some more.
> When you can't love anymore—
> find some quiet time
> to renew your soul and spirit.

## A SENSE OF PURPOSE

When you are "on purpose" there is an awareness of your boundaries and what you will and will not allow to happen. You can approach each day with a willingness to risk something new and to accept the consequences of your decisions. You are committed.

A willingness and commitment to change may be based on the realization you have a short time on Earth. There may be something you want to be remembered for, a contribution you want to make. So consider, if you had only six months to live, what would you do with your life? If you are not living your heart's desire—STOP! Look at the changes you could make in order to proceed towards your purpose.

The next question, then, is: "What do I really want to do with my life?"

The important distinction here is "want to" instead of "need to". "Want" is consideration of a longing or desire; "need" can cause you to collapse with weariness. It's very important to watch the words you use in your day-to-day lives. When you *need* to go to the grocery store, fill the car with gas, etc., you give up your power of choice and become a victim of circumstance.

You truly are in control of your decisions. You do not *have to* do anything. You don't *have* to get up in the

**73**

morning, we don't *have* to go to work, you don't *have* to return that phone call and you don't have to be on the job. Of course, there are consequences for each decision you make. From your decisions, you create new choices. Other options become available to you—new opportunities, new challenges.

Have you considered how different your life might be had you made different decisions? For example, being in a hurry much of the time, you get a speeding ticket. You have had a heavy foot in the past and this is your third speeding ticket. Now the insurance company is threatening to cancel your insurance. At the very least the premium will more than double, perhaps triple.

This money could have been used for two plane tickets to paradise. Or you could have tithed the money and perhaps changed someone's life forever. Different decisions bring about different experiences.

So as you think of "wanting to" instead of *needing to*, you can begin to redesign your life.

### LOVE IS...

*...being content with doing whatever is important to you*
*...calling someone just because you thought of them*
*...a pair of love birds amongst cherry blossoms*
*...seeing an artist's creation and two months later the*
*desire for painting is no less intense*
*...dreaming and knowing it will all come true*
*...friends*
*...a huge scoop of ice cream in a sugar cone*
*...reading and sharing, sharing and reading*
*...a sister you can tell off and it doesn't mean you don't*
*love her*
*...kids that come home to dinner*
*...dew on the lawn*
*...almond blossoms*
*...hugs, hugs and more hugs*

What is your true purpose for being in your current profession? When you applied for the position, you probably looked at the job description carefully, assessed your own qualifications and then went after the job with vigor and conviction. You knew this was the position that would benefit both you and the company.

*Why did I choose real estate?*

*Because it appeared glamorous! Successful realtors dress beautifully, wear wonderful jewelry, drive big cars, live in big homes and sometimes even become land barons (if they are risk takers)! Some have entered this field to learn the market and discover bargains. Still others wanted to be their own boss and be free from the constraints of an eight-to-five job. I thought money would make my dreams come true.*

To truly follow your dream, to strive for genuine self-actualization, you need to have the courage to dream, the courage to change.

Change can be scary and your own internal systems and your external relationships (personal as well as business) may work actively to avoid changes that are happening.

From your dream will come an awareness of your true purpose; a set of tools to help you to climb the mountain and reach the peak.

If this were the last day of your life...

✤ would you be reading this book?

✤ would you be holding a loved one?

✤ would you be at the ocean?

✤ would you be at work?

How grand life is when we can honestly say, "I'd be doing what I'm doing right *now*"—be it reading, eating, sleeping or working.

> Be complete with this one moment
> with no regrets, no excuses, no tomorrows.
>
> Be in touch with your deep power within —
> for this is the source of your strength.

## HAPPINESS

What would it take for your life to have both purpose and happiness?

It might mean letting go of the old ways of doing business, of living your life—letting go of the fantasy world you live in when you don't want to accept life the way it is.

It might mean giving up your stories because they don't work. For example, the stories about "why" the contract fell through, relating numerous "reasons" why it happened. The number of reasons you can come up with is only limited by your imagination.

The problem, however, is simple: the contract fell through. You see, as soon as you stop making someone or something wrong, the problem becomes very obvious and the issue isn't clouded with a lot of unnecessary garbage. When the real problem is presented, then possible solutions can be examined.

It might mean being willing to communicate in a way that stretches your comfort zone; or having the courage to take a stand.

## BIRDS

*Two black birds*
*A duet,*
*Creating harmony,*
*Making music,*
*Exploring the unknown.*
*One white bird,*
*Soaring freely,*
*Effortlessly,*
*With clarity and vision.*

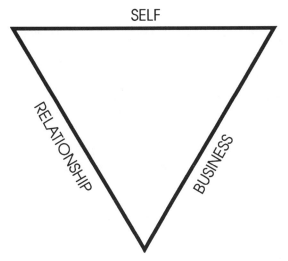

The base of the triangle is SELF. It is the foundation of all you do in your life—in business and relationships.

The second part of the triangle is labeled RELATIONSHIP, for without relationship, you have neither companionship or the ability to operate in business situations.

The third part is BUSINESS. One cannot do business in a vacuum. Notice the tip of the triangle has got a very fine point on it. It is very delicate and like a top it spins when there is momentum. But when there is no movement or interaction, the top topples.

We often find it difficult to achieve a delicate balance.

Happiness comes with enjoying whatever you have and letting it be enough. Make room for the new, let go of the old and accept what is.

Then, if you were to die tomorrow, you would have no regrets.

### KNOWING

*Just when I think I know, I no longer know. New worlds open up, new vistas appear, new knowledge confronts me.*

*I spend my days integrating the material I have just learned. I am in a pipe line, moving quickly. It seems a whole new community has opened up to me. I've learned there are people like me in every walk of life.*

*The truth is I am healing from a lifetime of self-abuse. I am well and healthy, and it's important to keep my eyes open yet see through my heart.*

*I have become a scholar, a writer. I am learning self-love on a new, gentle and exciting level. My days go by quickly. I am ready to move on.*

*I am still the same person I've always been, only now I know I have an inner light and I am a child of God. I move forward, always letting go or letting grow.*

*When I let things be, I am happy and free.*

To move towards happiness, to truly let go, means giving up all attachments to people, places and things. It means emptying yourself completely, becoming totally devoid of every thought and feeling, almost like deprivation. Then turn the deprivation into gratitude. Once you fill nothingness with gratitude and serenity, you can then take a fresh look at your awareness, willingness and commitment.

*Part 4*

# THE ADVENTURE—RISK

**Chapter 7**
**RISK**

**Chapter 8**
**TRUST**

**Chapter 9**
**CHOICES**

*Chapter 7*

# RISK

*The Truth
Risking Relationship
Ridicule, Rejection and Reprimand
Balance*

---

It's only when you can take the ultimate risk
in your personal life,
that you can then take the ultimate risk
in your business life.

---

*This is the chapter you learn about the fourth step of the
paradigm, RISK.*

## RISK

Risk-taking is letting it be okay to attain your own
magnificence. It involves action which you might
think leads to danger or the exposure of danger. Whether
you are climbing a mountain, buying a new car or house,
cleaning up old relationships or beginning new ones, the
element of fear can enter.

## CHANGE

*How do I feel?*
*My tummy is tickling.*
*My blood is rushing and gushing through my veins.*
*I feel light-headed,*
*yet my feet are planted firmly on the ground.*
*I feel like singing, yet I am listening.*
*I am choosing excitement rather than anxiety.*
*The flower is opening.*

A personal risk can be as grandiose as a trip to Africa or as simple as making a call to an alienated friend.

Risk-taking on the personal level is asking for what you want—and being prepared to not receive it, knowing it doesn't make either of you wrong.

There is the fine line between not making someone wrong and taking the blame yourself. A healthy response would be to tell the truth as to how it is for you at the moment. Letting the other person know the feelings are yours and have nothing to do with them. This takes a bit of practice but the rewards are tremendous!

*Sometime ago, I was asked by a friend, "Who are you?" I replied, "I'm a speaker who's afraid to speak, I'm a writer who's afraid to write, I'm a singer who's afraid to sing, I'm about love and afraid to love."*

*I was also asked to think of one word, one thing, one common element, that was superimposed on everything I do. I thought about all the words important to me and the one that kept ringing true was Risk.*

*It was at this moment, I again heard the words of Helen Keller. "Life is either a daring adventure or nothing." It was at this moment I heard the words of Erica Jong, "And the trouble is, if you risk nothing, you risk even more." It was at this*

**81**

*moment I remembered the painting of the rose by an artist friend—a metaphorical portrait of myself.*

When is the last time you took a risk in business? When was the last time you took a risk with your family? Your friends? With yourself? Are you ready for your life to be different? Are you ready to break out of the box, your self-imposed barriers, that keep you stuck in the dance step?

**FRIENDS...**

...*believe in you when you no longer believe in yourself.*
...*love you when you thought you no longer knew what the word meant.*
...*let you cry and assure you all is well.*
...*think you are super and special just the way you are.*
...*tell you how beautiful you are when you can see no beauty.*
...*speak their truth, even when you don't want to hear it.*
...*enjoy quiet moments together when words aren't necessary.*
...*let you love them, too.*

---

The more I risk without fear,
the more I speak the truth
as it is for me,
the further and faster I go on my path.

---

## THE TRUTH

One of the ways to take risks is to tell the truth.
When you don't tell the truth as it is for you, you become a victim. With each little "white lie" you begin to

distance yourself from yourself and others. Feelings of frustration, anger and resentment may cloud your mind. The body then begins to feel discomfort.

Honesty is also listening to what your body is trying to tell you. It's listening to the tightening in the shoulders, the throbbing in the temples, the stress in the lower back. It's listening to the feelings that manifest themselves in the way of "dis-ease" in the body.

Next time you notice your body shutting down, try asking yourself: "What is the message my body is trying to give me?" "What have I done outside my integrity?" "What can I do in order to handle these body sensations and relax my body?"

*My biggest challenge has been to trust myself to know that what I'm doing is exactly as it must be.*

Be clear about what you want, then speak clearly about your desires.

Answer the following questions, keeping the answer simple. Allow whatever comes up for you to be so. Pretend you can only have one thing: i.e. success, happiness, relationship, children, health, wealth, etc.

- ✤ What do I want?
- ✤ What am I willing to give?
- ✤ What am I willing to receive?
- ✤ What am I willing to ask for?
- ✤ What am I willing to let go of in order to make room for what I want?

Let's say that what you want is success at work. You are willing to give time and energy in order to achieve this. You are willing to ask for assistance. You are willing to receive help from others. You are willing to hear what you might not want to hear.

Tell your truth and be open to other people's truth. And be willing to let go of the job, if that is what is necessary. This is the key to success.

> Risking is doing whatever you haven't done
> that you want to do.

### SUPPORT

*You carried me when I couldn't walk*
*You stayed with me*
*when others couldn't handle my tantrums.*
*You were always beside me,*
*believing, trusting,*
*having faith.*

*You saw my dimmed inner light*
*which flickered and threatened to go out.*
*You saw who I was*
*and who I am now becoming.*
*You encouraged me, loved me,*
*gave me a safe place*
*to be when I couldn't face myself.*

*You opened your heart to me*
*like you have to none other.*
*I can truly say, you are the one.*
*The one that reached out*
*and risked "all out"*
*to save me from the quicksand*
*of my own mind and soul.*

*Yes, it is because of you—*
*that stretch of your finger tips,*
*until they touched mine.*

*That allowed me to open my rose,*
*to share love, light and discoveries.*

**84**

> Your heart belongs to you...
> who you give it to and for how long,
> is your choice alone to make.

## RISKING RELATIONSHIP

*There was a time in my life when I was undergoing a lot of change. People who love me—my family to be specific—were concerned and frightened about the changes I was making. In particular, my sons felt a strong need to take care of me and tell me what I should be doing.*

*Many times this would happen during telephone conversations. I felt powerful feelings in my body. It was feelings of helplessness. It was anger! It was rage!*

*I considered my options, like yelling, arguing or screaming, or pushing down the tremendous power surging through my body. Instead, I calmly hung up the phone! This took some risk!! And certainly was a new way of handling confrontation.*

*The freedom that came with the severing of the phone connection was almost indescribable. It was total release.*

So what is risk-taking in relationship? What happens when you risk letting the other person know just who you truly are, what you like and what you don't like?

It's very difficult to take risks in relationship. It takes a lot of courage to tell your mother it doesn't work for you to be with her on her birthday. It takes courage to tell someone you love what does and doesn't work for you. It takes a lot of courage to calmly hang up the phone. As with everything else, there are costs and benefits when we take risks in personal relationships.

**85**

To be in relationship means to be connected. We are in relationship with every person we know and meet. Some of us like to think we are only in relationship with those we choose. The truth is, we are connected to every other human being on some level.

*Some time ago I was in my car, stopped at a stop sign. My attention went to the neighboring car. The driver was a handsome man in a business suit. He was giving me a big smile and a wave. I felt myself begin to flush. Like a young girl, I turned shyly away.*

*I wondered what it meant. I began to make up all kinds of stories about this innocent smile and wave. Many times over the year, this incident has flashed through my mind.*

*Since I enjoyed this brief encounter immensely, I decided to risk a little. I began to make eye contact with other drivers, passengers and children. What I found were faces eager to return my smile and wave. Children played peek-a-boo with me. I got big grins from the younger drivers, truckers honked and a tremendous amount of joy was exchanged in these brief encounters.*

*This was the gift of the "Smiling Man".*

You have heard, "The eye is the window to the soul." Try *using* this as fact. Look your business associates in the eye, with the intent to hear clearly what they are saying. What the listeners hear and the speaker says, are not always the same. This eye contact will allow you to see, hear and understand at a deeper lever of communication. It's like hearing with your heart instead of your ears.

## BROTHERHOOD

*To love one another—all others—every day,*
*every minute.*
*To see beauty in a woman whom you don't know—one*
*who radiates the beauty and doesn't even know it. You tell*
*her how beautiful she is.*
*To see the innocent look in a child's eye—the vast depth of*
*knowingness, yet he looks in search of what he does not*
*know. Smile and let him see your love.*

*To dance with another, to hear and feel the heart beat, the*
*rhythm of the music, the blending of two bodies for brief,*
*innocent moments. And to know all that has transpired is a*
*pleasant exchange.*

*To appreciate the gentle nature of a cat—*
*the one that privileges us with her presence and demands*
*attention at will.*
*To hear all creatures, see all creatures,*
*love all creatures.*
*Brotherhood.*

People are flattered to know you want and actually demand clear communication. Be rigorous when it comes to communication. Be willing to be sure you've heard and understood the instructions, the message or the communication correctly.

This sounds so easy. You might say, "This is elementary." Yes! It is elementary. And how many times in one day, perhaps even one hour, do you walk away, shaking your head, disappointed at what you hoped to accomplish in working with another? How many times do you throw up your hands in despair and attempt to give up? How many times do you say, it just isn't worth it? How many times do you quit?

Saying what must be said is one way of ensuring you are always ready for today to be the last day of your (or their) life.

Risking relationship at home might involve telling your mate you just bought four new dresses. It means being willing to accept responsibility for your actions and choices. And letting your decisions be okay!

Risking relationship at home might be in telling your significant other you are choosing to play golf instead of being with her… and not feeling guilty.

Risking relationship might be to tell a child, not even your own, how precious they are.

Risking relationship might be to tell a parent or friend whatever needs to be said in order to let old dis-agreements, trials and tribulations go by the wayside.

It means being willing to accept responsibility for your actions and choices and not let your decisions be wrong.

> When people really hear
> what you are saying,
> it will likely bring tears.

## EARLY SPRING—BEFORE DAWN

*The sky, shades of pastel pink and blue*
*Mist, hanging on the pond as if by magic*
*The birch trees, barren*
*Graced only with an occasional bunch of mistletoe*

*A crow perched, here and there, atop a pine*
*Keeping watch over his world.*
*My mind moved swiftly from my outer world of reality*
*To the inner sanctum of my heart*
*Blessed with the ability to see the total picture*
*Yet cursed by the same blessing*
*I wonder what is….*

*My mind creates chaos in an attempt to sort.*
*Assumptions—my downfall*
*The blessing—my curse*
*My mind completes the circle of possibilities*
*Gathering evidence appropriate for each degree*
*Confusion surfaces and grows in abundance*
*Allowing no space for distinction between reality*
*and fantasy.*
*My heart is delicate—vulnerable*
*Knowing now what heartache is about*
*Having felt the pain—and the gain*
*I wonder if I should ask….*
*Knowing if I don't, there may be no possibility*
*Yet if I do—I may create an opening…*
*For a Love of which I have never known.*
*Will I risk?*

> Ridicule and Recognition:
> The fear of one
> and the need for the other.
> How to let go of both.

## RIDICULE, REJECTION AND REPRIMAND

Taking risks involves the possibility of being ridiculed, rejected or reprimanded.

*There's a little restaurant in Vancouver, Canada, called Sophie's Cosmic Cafe. It is a favoured spot for breakfast. Even on a rainy weekday there may be a wait. The meals are reasonably priced, tasty, large and promptly served.*

*What makes Sophie's so remarkable, though, is the outlandish decor of this establishment. The walls are decorated with a variety of Fifties memorabilia. One wall has a pool table mounted with a game in progress.*

*In addition, the owner is outlandish. Sophie is an average looking, middle-aged woman with greying hair who dares to go all out. She will dress in a baggy black dress and black tennis shoes; she sports white stockings with musical notations in black and red—clefs, triplets, sharps and flats adorn her legs. She is willing to risk being ridiculed or rejected. Yet what she gets is more business.*

Fear often accompanies risk. What you may fear is the loss of control over the outcome. Acknowledge the fear, remember your purpose and transform your fear-energy into excitement.

Sometimes the fear is more like terror, and paralysis sets in! It's possible to feel like a trapped rabbit who has no place to hide when an eagle is circling overhead—to feel that all safety is gone.

This terror is actually due to projecting into the future. When you stay with what is happening right now, fear has no place. It's when you visualize and experience the future on a body level that you get into trouble.

An exercise that helps to deal with this fear is to mentally move into the fearful situation. As you imagine the worst scenario, notice your body reactions. Notice if your heart is pounding. Notice your breathing—if it is shallow. In your imagination, you can approach or retreat from this fearful experience.

You can return to the present at any time as the situation becomes too intense. Again, mentally approach the scene of conflict or fear. Breathe and calm your body until you can access this place in your mind with ease and gentleness. Keep breathing deeply.

I have used this powerful exercise to assist others who were experiencing fear in their various situations, including a person in divorce negotiations; a singer conquering stage fright; a teacher dealing with an irate parent; and many other business transactions.

Being afraid can stop you from doing whatever you are doing. You may become angry, feel taken advantage of or become a victim. You may feel you have no choice. Then, like the rabbit, you are trapped, paralyzed.

---

There comes a time when we are so far into it—
whatever "it" is—
that we cannot retreat easily.
At that point we have to
let it go or let it grow.

---

## A JOURNEY IN LIFE

*I'm sitting in a triangular tub.*
*I'm on my way to the moon.*
*The tub is redwood and reinforced*
*with the strongest metal known.*
*It's got no top and it's got no bottom*
*Just the angular sides.*

*The ride is exciting, exhilarating...*
*and windy and cold as hell.*
*The sides of the tub are labeled*
*Purpose, Pride and Promise.*
*The tub keeps turning and I'm never sure*
*Which side will next be my base.*

*Is it Purpose without which I am nothing?*
*Is it Pride in who I am?*
*Is it Promise of life*
*With harmony, peace and grace?*
*I love the ride, I love the freedom*
*Yet Ease is not a part of the package.*
*To prove myself is what they want,*
*It's not designed for all to win.*
*This whole journey smacks of abuse*
*The pushing, the pulling, the tugging*
*The shoving, reframing, remaking*
*Removing, reuniting, recreating*

*I feel tired.*
*Like a housewife acknowledged only for sex*
*And the person she is in totality*
*Is not a part of the whole.*

*What is for me next?*
*Have I felt all the elements?*
*Have there been enough clouds and storms?*
*Is sunshine just around the corner?*
*Or is this a fantasy I have designed*
*That I'm calling my life?*

**92**

*What are my options?*
*What are my desires?*
*The triangular tub and I*
*Set out on a journey to the moon.*
*Could it be that I'm already there*
*And I don't even know it?*

There are costs in moving relationships to a deeper level. It may mean risking rejection, ridicule, resentment and reprimands. It means some people won't like you. It might mean people in your circle of friends and friendly co-workers no longer want to be around you. Some of these people are not willing to hear, to see, to be heard or to be seen.

The challenge for you is to let them be as they are in their not-hearing-not-seeing mode and still respect them. The challenge for you is to keep connecting with other people—to choose a support team. You see, when you decide you want to move relationships to a different level, everything in your life will change.

The truth of the matter is, no matter what you say or do, you can still experience rejection. You may still experience ridicule. You may still experience reprimands. So you see, you risk nothing when you risk relationship. Your only choices are the insanity circle or breaking out of the insanity circle—breaking through.

> It takes you to win for me to win.

# BALANCE

In any relationship, there is a desire for balance. If you are sitting on a teeter-totter with a person of unequal weight, considerable negotiation is necessary to balance.

The balancing process is one of slow, steady, planned movements. It requires communication and constant little adjustments.

Balance involves finding the extremes of the "too many—not enough" dichotomy. Since nature abhors a vacuum, when a time or relationship space is created, nature returns an abundance of choices.

### OKAY

*Is it really okay for things to be okay?*
*I feel crazy—yet my mind is still.*
*I feel giddy—yet my body is still.*
*I feel frightened—yet I'm safe and secure.*
*I feel loved—yet I'm not sure it's okay.*
*Is it really going to come true?*
*All of my wishes, dreams, hopes, visions?*
*Is it okay that my life be filled with joy, hope, love and laughter?*
*Why these feelings? Why this glow?*
*Why this discontent when I know it's so?*
*Just because...*
*This is the way it is!*

# Chapter 8

# TRUST

*Confidence*

Make mistakes—
and learn to recover quickly,
like an Aikido master.

*Trust is the fifth step in the paradigm for change.*

## CONFIDENCE

### FOCUS

*This winter season of my life
will be a time of tranquility, rest and peace.
It will be a renewal for the activity of spring.
I am assimilating and integrating the knowledge,
understanding the wisdom of the earth
and the sages thereof.
I am moving at warp speed to higher plateaus
where the air is pure and crystal,
grasses are vibrant with life and color,
the flowers are of indescribable delicate beauty and grace.
They wave, beckoning for me to smell their sweetness,
and to remind me of my purpose on this Earth:
to be here fully each moment,
fearing neither the future nor the past.
My present is to be at peace with myself, therefore with all
others.*

**95**

Winter is the season of trust. Everything looks barren and asleep, yet beneath the cold snow lie numerous seeds of life. Soon, as if by magic, buds will appear on the trees. The bear will emerge from its cave.

Trust is often defined as being able to place confidence in a relationship. You have heard the words, "Trust me. I will take care of you." or "Trust me, you are in good hands." These words bring to my mind a poster of a young cat with it's paw just above a gold fish bowl. Underneath the picture are the words, "Trust me."

*When I hear these words, an alarm goes off in my head. You see, the only one in whom confidence can be placed is myself. In any relationship the only real condition of trust is the ability to trust in oneself.*

*When I go to climb a mountain, I am the one ultimately responsible for my own life. I must trust myself to feel secure with my team players as we prepare to ascend the mountain.*

When you trust, you surrender to your intuitive self. Your physical body feels a release of tension. You are confident and at ease. You relinquish control over the outcome. That big C word. *Control.*

When you trust yourself, you make the correct decision, regardless of the outcome. There are lessons and gifts that come with every decision. Eventually when you have had enough lessons and you have learned whatever it was you were to learn, you begin to receive the gifts.

Ultimately, it doesn't matter which decision you make. In the book, *Alice In Wonderland*, the Cheshire Cat explained it to Alice. "The way you go depends on where you want to go, and if you don't know where you are going, then it won't matter which road you take."

It is important to take "time-outs"—time to realign your goals and direction. One of the challenges of the journey of life is knowing and trusting yourself to stop as necessary in order to realign.

The gifts come quicker and quicker. This happens when you are willing to get the point of the lesson sooner, before it becomes painful or dysfunctional. You will go through your feelings and emotions no matter where you are, if you have chosen a path of growth.

Go and do what your heart
and soul dictates.
Be in touch
with your deep power within—
for this is the source of your strength.

Have faith. Faith in yourself to make the correct decision. Have faith like Edison, who didn't give up after thousands of tries, because he knew that he could create an incandescent light bulb. Have faith like Beethovan, who wrote some of his most powerful music after his hearing was completely gone. Have faith like Martin Luther King, who had a dream and lived it.

## THE DAY THE KITES FLEW

*The sun was warming to the bones. The air was fresh with gentle summer breezes. The sky—clear blue with traces of high wispy clouds. Then in tandem appeared white and blue with the red maple leaf—a harmony of birds attached to a string. The pair flew with precision and grandeur, quivering in the breeze, with intentionality.*

*Suddenly, the kites appeared, not more than a few feet away, as if from nowhere, hovering, alive with vitality. They came diving from the heavens, honoring and saluting the audience of two.*

*I felt the magnificence of the skill, acquired through more than a decade of practice. The dedication and concentration was clear. The rewards—pleasing others, competitions, but most of all joy in the knowledge that patience and persistence bring huge benefits.*

*Chapter 9*

# CHOICES

---

| Choices are the heart and soul of life. |

*The final step!*

## CHOICE

Have you ever felt that you have too many choices? When there are too many decisions to make, you become overwhelmed and confused. Do you stop caring about the results and just want to "get it over with"?

When you feel there are no options, do you feel boxed in and lose your creativity?

When I hear someone say "I had no choice," or "There was no other way," I listen to their pain. They have started to close down to life and need support in looking at other options. You see, it's when we can brainstorm for solutions that the life force again surges through our body.

Perhaps you know someone or some company that has gone through bankruptcy. Do they say, "We had no choice!" instead of, "This was the best option"?

It is our failure to recognize our choices which keeps us asleep, unconscious, out of touch with reality.

You only have to make one choice at a time.

Choices to live or die, to sleep or be awake, to love and be loved, or to despise and be despised are yours for as little cost as a flicker of the mind. They are as simple as setting a dial on a radio and possibly as difficult as reading the instruction manual on how to set the dial. Awareness is the key. Once there is awareness, many options are revealed.

### CHOOSING

*What is this childlike tug, relentlessly urging me to do what is unnecessary?*

*Today I begin a new day. Today I will do exactly as I choose. I am no longer a victim, waiting for family, friends or loved ones to make this day wonderful for me. This day is wonderful! I am vibrantly alive, blessed and free. I do exactly as I want. There is no other person who can do for me what I can do for myself. I design my life. I am totally and completely responsible for the outcome of each day, hour, moment. I am filled with the breath of life, the power of love and the miracle of being. I have unlimited opportunities available to me. I need only open the doors and walk through. Today I am opening more doors and I enter each room, filled with courage, confidence and humility.*

An important way to make decisions is to weigh the costs and the benefits. For example, you may be considering a job change. The immediate cost might be loss of security. The visible benefit might be a greater sense of fulfillment. But in the long run, there may be no difference at all.

What are the costs of waking up?

❖ You might experience growth, and with growth comes discomfort or emotional pain.

❖ Life will never be the same again!

❖ You might create breakdown.

✤ You might sell your company.

✤ You might quit your job.

✤ You might divorce your spouse.

What might be some of the benefits of waking up?

✤ You might experience growth, and with growth comes joy.

✤ Life will never be the same.

✤ There will be breakthrough after breakthrough.

✤ You might sell your company.

✤ You might quit your job.

✤ You might divorce your spouse.

You see, the benefits and costs are the same. It's just like the old adage of the half-full glass of water or the half-empty glass. It's all a matter of perspective. See the half-full glass and the half-empty glass!

And since the costs and benefits are the same, why not choose openness and life instead of loss of power and an eventual slow death?

---

Is this just another adventure? Another distraction?
Will I still get where I am going?

---

Every day of your life, every minute, you are making choices. Mundane as weighing out the consequences of returning or not returning phone calls—or as important as deciding to buy a house. You look at the choices. What

**101**

will be the consequences of each choice and what is best for me? If you are aware, the choices are there.

It's like a rabbit running from the shadow of an eagle. It returns to its burrow, only to find a snake lying in the entrance. Paralysis sets in, as the rabbit feels it has no choices. But in reality, it has several options, if it can only break out of the box and look for them. There may be scrub it can hide in. There may be an alternate entrance to the burrow.

When you are locked into survival, you see no choices. When you can trust that you have possibilities, you do.

It really boils down to being responsible for your actions, your intentions, your life—every day and every minute. It is being willing to accept the consequences of your decisions—the outcomes.

### RAMBLINGS

*The magical, musical moments of the journey to the ocean, via the redwoods. An indescribable euphoria of joy and bliss. Leaves of gold, rust, burgundy and brown cling to the twigs and branches.*

*The bark of the deciduous trees is magnificently displayed amongst the redwoods, cedars and evergreens. The hills and valleys have a thin veil of mist spread so delicately as to only give an aura of the supernatural.*

*I am filled once again with the wonder of life.*

*The sunlight streams through the powerful dark green trees, leaving a new awareness of the brilliance of life, love. Quiet moments, our eternity to share or hoard as we choose.*

*Even the earth is beautiful. The dark grey taupe of the bare soils emits a perfect readiness for new life to spring forth. The moisture will come and in time the seed carried or deposited by bird, reptile or soft, scurrying creature.*

*Dark shadows of the mid-day in a forest are reminiscent of childhood years of freedom, carefree and limitless—a freedom often lost in adulthood. Shadows through the sagging branches make musical sounds of chimes, flutes and harps. Voices of angels singing haunting melodies filled with the harmony of nature, life and tranquility.*

*Observe the excitement and strength of the eternal now. A peek into the beauty and solitude of the future. What is uniqueness? Dichotomy is balance. The extreme of what is nature, life, love.*

*Breaking forth—*
*Explosion of brilliant colors radiating from the prism just as the petals of the flower have their own unique and personal hues, size, shape. The twittering of birds and rustling furry creatures make me feel alive, energized, excited.*

*Windy weather, blowing golden sand.*
*Waves are rough, like a pot of boiling porridge.*
*White capped waves*
*Shallow water,*
*Tossing and swirling beads of fine sand.*

*Then murky edges*
*graduate to various shades*
*of yellow-green, blue-green,*
*to the beautiful midnight blue.*

*Sounds of moving water*
*totally in control,*
*Wind moving swiftly past my ears.*

*The tie that binds—telling the truth, risking rejection, risking loving, creates an opening for nature (which is all) to touch me, you, us. A oneness of all with all—the universe.*

*PART 5*

# THE DANCE—TIME, ENERGY, MONEY

**Chapter 10**
**TIME, ENERGY, MONEY**

**Chapter 11**
**SCARCITY**

**Chapter 12**
**ABUNDANCE**

**Chapter 13**
**NEEDS**

# TIME, ENERGY, MONEY

> There are two kinds of time:
> TIMELESSNESS: what is, intuitive,
> uncommitted, unstructured, creation. A river
> flowing with ease and grace.
>
> STRUCTURED TIME: the commitment,
> responsibility, your word, your action. A solid
> structure where change occurs slowly and
> painstakingly.

Time is all you have. It is the greatest gift you can give. Everyone has the same amount of time. You have enough if you say you do.

### THE PRESENT

*All there is for me is the present.*
*I will look to the future for my visions.*
*I will look to the past for my gifts.*
*I will live today in the moment*
*and allow the light and love*
*of the universe to shine through me.*

*While attending a workshop some time ago, I saw how my lack of time was directly tied to my fear of missing out on something. The "something" was an exercise class, meditation, breakfast, lunch or a quiet walk along the beach.*

*It didn't really seem to matter what the activity was or wasn't—I just seemed to scurry, faster and faster. I was always trying to include everything so I would lose nothing.*

*The result of this frenzy was the realization that in the fear of missing "something" I miss all.*

> Energy is your life force.

# ENERGY AND MONEY

E nergy comes from the sun, the earth, the universe. You can monitor your energy. You can manipulate the flow and make tiny changes to enhance your store of energy. Sleep and rest helps your body replenish energy. Food and water add new energy. As you become conscious of the types of substances you put into your body, you are better able to adjust your energy. Breathing—deep breathing—enhances the use of energy throughout your system.

> Money is a commodity that we buy
> with time and energy.

M oney is no more than pieces of paper. So much importance is attached to it! Self-worth and success are often measured by money. Others are judged by their attitude towards money. Money buys privileges, and thus it appears to be the source of happiness, and sadness is linked to the lack of it.

Much time is spent earning money. It is assumed that the more one has the better off one is. Money creates uncomfortable situations. Thinking about the future—security, pensions, retirement—makes it seem that life revolves around money.

Balancing time, energy and money is another constant challenge. Time is your most precious commodity. You can use time to increase your energy (by exercise or sleep, for example, depending on if you need to rev up or quiet down). You can use time to increase your money or decrease it, depending on whether you are earning or spending.

Time is what makes relationships work: relationships with oneself, family and friends, and the world.

### WORRY

*I feel like I'm caught in the grips of fear*
*Almost to the point of being paralyzed.*
*I'm worried about finances,*
*Creating income vs outgo.*
*I push myself harder and harder,*
*Demanding more and more of myself.*
*Sometimes I feel like I'm going to crack.*
*What's next for me is to focus—*
*Take one step at a time.*

# SCARCITY

> All you have is time—
> time to give wherever you choose.

## SCARCITY OF TIME

In the business world, many times it seems there aren't enough hours in the day for all the "things" that need to be done—time to do paper work, answer the phone, deal with correspondence, time to meet with the big account, time to delegate, time to design a strategy and time to handle the unforeseen problems that come up unexpectedly every day.

Families seem to want more and more of your time, too. The kids need rides to school, piano lessons, soccer practice, the swim team.

Groceries need to be purchased, hair cut, bills paid, and the auto filled with gas. Spouses hope to have a little time to talk and play together.

Should you be lucky enough to still have your parents alive, they'd appreciate some time too. Sometimes they don't understand what you do with your time. You can't answer that question yourself, since you don't know where it goes either.

Everyone wants some personal time. Time to sing, dance, climb mountains, visit with friends or read a book; time to exercise and be alone; time to celebrate that big deal you just locked up; a time to rest, meditate or pray.

You want time for a time out.

## ON BEING ALONE

*Time to reflect on what is really important.*
*Time to rest, be quiet and still.*
*Time to read words of wisdom.*
*Perhaps time to write some, too.*
*Time to draw pictures of flowers,*
*Time to see if I still like myself.*
*Time to feel the feelings—*
*Whatever may come up.*
*Time to listen to my body,*
*To check in—pay attention.*
*Time to love myself,*
*Live with myself,*
*Be with myself.*
*Time to let God in.*

You may have taken time management courses, read time management books and purchased and filled out the newest day planner. Has it really made a dent in your time schedule?

Time management courses teach how to cut the pie into more or different pieces. But there still remains the quandary of not having enough time. It seems there are not enough hours in the day.

Are you aware of where you spend your time? Every hour of every day?

**110**

Do you know an average person who lives to be 70 years old has spent 23 years of their life asleep? Another 16 years of their life is spent at work. That leaves 31 years eating, dressing, traveling, being sick, staying healthy, reading, watching TV and being in relationship.

---

Master interruptions and distractions,
lest they master you.
You can always let something
stop you from succeeding.

---

## PEOPLE-PLEASING

People-pleasing holds you back from being successful. It allows you to be a victim. You allow friends to distract you from what you are doing.

Most of the time people do the things that reward them. The rewards can have a definite benefit at the physical, mental and spiritual levels. But, every action also brings costs in terms of time, energy or money. What then are the costs and benefits of people-pleasing?

People-pleasing is giving to another or others at the expense of yourself. It is distinctly different from service. Service is giving to another because of the desire to do so, with no expectation of repayment and no obligation. The doing is the reward.

People-pleasing is committing to others and then wishing you hadn't. It's doing for others without checking in with yourself to know whether it works for you. It gives you the excuse to be ineffective, non-productive and deficient in time and energy.

**111**

People-pleasing is excused by a desire to not hurt anyone. The challenge is to be courageous, break out of the trap, to come out of hiding, to do what works for you. There is no guarantee you will never cause anyone injury, but your intention is to not hurt others either physically or emotionally.

Often the people-pleasing role is jumped into unconsciously. It's kind of like reacting with a "Sure, okay," instead of with a "Yes, I'd like to do that. It will work for me." People-pleasing happens frequently among family members and friends both at home and in the workplace.

> The costs of pleasing others at the expense of oneself
> can far outweigh the benefits
> in more ways than time and energy and money.

*My mother, who is now in her 80's is excited when her brother, who lives in Montana, comes to Reno on a gaming flight. She asks if I will take her there for the day. Now, Reno is a five-to-six-hour round trip by car over the Sierra Nevada Mountains. And this is in the summer when weather conditions are good.*

*One wintery February day, I was asked to drive her to Reno. I had a seven-hour gap in my schedule and wanting to please my mom, we started out for the mountains. She was so anxious to see her brother, that one or two hours with him was much better than nothing.*

*What happened? We hit black ice! If you have ever hit black ice, you know you have no control over your car. The car started skating and sliding! It spun around three times and ended up against the center railing!*

*I knew in my heart I had no business attempting this journey. All my reasoning screamed "NO!" My intuitive self said "NO!" Yet, I didn't listen. I needed to learn this lesson one more time.*

*I still had not gotten the message to trust myself. I chose to please my mom and endangered both our lives in the process. Luckily, only the car was damaged. An expensive lesson, yet perhaps a cheap one.*

People-pleasing can waste and even cost lives. When you fail to trust your own innermost self, little by little you die. The vibrant, excited, decisive self begins to close down. This is the beginning of "dis-ease", which causes disease, and sometimes a very slow, painful death.

Dramatic costs! This book is about taking responsibility for your life. It's about waking up to the ways in which you trick yourself. No one else is affected the way you are by your decisions. Yet, those around you can be affected in both positive and negative ways.

When you don't take the responsibility for your own life, you usually have to make up excuses, justifying the reasons why your life isn't working out.

Most importantly, we are models for our children, our parents, our friends, our colleagues. Who we are lights or dims the way for those we love.

Some ways we people-please are:

❖ We eat food we don't like.

❖ We second guess in order to get approval.

❖ We put up with unacceptable behavior.

❖ We change our schedules.

❖ We alter our environment.

❖ We listen to inane chatter when we don't want to.

❖ We change our whole life style.

**113**

In addition to the cost in time, pleasing others at the expense of yourself depletes your life force, energy.

Passengers on an airplane are told to put the oxygen mask on themselves first in case of an emergency, and only after it is in place should they put one on their children. If you don't take care of yourself first and foremost, you can't be effectively around to care for others.

The distinction between being selfish and caring for yourself can indeed be a difficult one. Caring for yourself involves checking in to know what is authentic for the moment.

---

I will go to any lengths to avoid doing
certain things.
I will use any means to avoid going where I really
want to go.

---

# PROCRASTINATION AND DISTRACTION

*I burn so much energy thinking about the project at hand! Why do I procrastinate so? Anything will distract me—a phone call I just received, books scattered here and there, or the classical music tape which so inspires me and has just ended.*

*I know I need to focus, to concentrate fully on the task at hand; I know I should delegate. But what about the dead roses on the desk? Couldn't I concentrate more fully if I had fresh flowers? And the coffee is cold, the mail just arrived and I have so many incoming calls!*

*I can go on and on! I've tried lists, doing the high priority items first. But somehow the little items hang on and take my energy. They clutter my mind and prevent me from focusing on the project.*

Clutter! How many of us work around clutter? We've all heard, "A cluttered environment makes for a cluttered mind." Check out the top of your desk, your files, your desk drawers. Check out the clutter in your home.

Check out the reasons you give for not taking care of it. Again, more rationalizations, more excuses, more justifications. More precious energy being burnt until you collapse into bed exhausted from what you get done!

What then is the purpose of keeping the clutter? You know the cost, but what is the benefit?

The question that needs to be asked is, "Can I risk getting rid of the clutter?" Examine the costs and benefits in time, energy and money that would result from getting rid of it and making life simpler.

If you wait too long to complete a task it becomes a "have to"—a project no longer of your own choice. Then you become a victim, trying to place the blame on extraneous circumstances as to why you haven't done what you set out to do.

The time lost in procastination is gone forever. The niggering worry of a job not done draws on your energy and robs you of peace of mind.

Once you focus on the project at hand, you will find that the relief at getting it started is so great that the job is done before you know it. The reward of accomplishment is well worth the effort and letting go of the clutter in your life leaves spacious room to breathe and a clear view of your priorities.

> Take time to be well...
> or you will take time to be sick.

# SCARCITY OF ENERGY AND MONEY

Some of you keep going even when you are low on energy. You have a quota to meet. There are meetings scheduled that you must attend. You have bills to pay, children to raise, places to go and people to see. But you deplete your energy resources by not listening to your bodies when exercise, rest or food is necessary. You are depleted by worry and blame. You tense up and forget to breathe. You begin to feel the scarcity of energy and time.

*It is time to refuel!*

Energy gives you capacity to accomplish all that you wish to do. Everyone has a different energy level, be aware of yours. That energy level must be replenished with food, rest and spiritual upliftment. Therefore, listen not just to your body but your mind and your spirit. When you run low on energy, you are not living efficiently.

When it comes to money, are you ever sure when enough is enough? It seems everyone wants more and more. Even millionaires want more and they are willing to take enormous risks to increase their net worth. However, many do not put much energy towards their own happiness.

Others, like many spiritual leaders such as Peace Pilgrim, Ghandi and Jesus disclaimed money and personal possessions. Yet their needs were always met.

If life is no longer working for you, its time to take stock and look at your priorities.

☐ Do you have enough money to meet your needs?

☐ How do you spend your money?

☐ Are you living your life the way you want to?

☐ Does more of your energy go into making money?

☐ Do you use your energy to create happiness?

The opposite of scarcity is abundance. In order to have abundance you first must be aware that you are coming from scarcity. Then, look at your willingness to have life be different and continue through the paradigm to choices. Look at your options.

Remember, the first step in resolving a scarcity issue is to realize you are in scarcity. More on this topic will follow in the next chapter.

> Whenever I feel more than,
> I am also less than.

## BEING IN ENVY

For the past four decades our society has been dedicated to the acquisition of "more." We feel that our identity is defined by our possessions—our houses, our cars, our degrees and so on.

This "need" for more, coupled with an ego-attachment to possessions, is part of the "never enough" syndrome, and it can take us into painful emotional places.

A short excursion through the dictionary reveals a lot about jealousy and envy. Envy is defined as a *painful or resentful awareness of an advantage enjoyed by another*

**117**

person, together with a desire to possess the same advantage.

Similarly, jealousy involves hostility, distrust and suspicion towards a rival or someone whom we feel has an advantage.

Hostility, suspicion, distrust—none of these are healthy feelings. When you become resentful, you usually become indignant, and being indignant implies a loss of dignity.

Envy comes from not being able to be grateful for what you already have. When you are envious, you tend to look on others with disapproval or distrust. The object of your jealousy gains power over you. You start to seek ways to obtain an advantage you desire—to take it away from whomever has it. And in doing so, you make the other person better than you are. Then the "Poor me!" attitude shows up. It is another "I'd be happy if..." situation.

When you are jealous, you seek to be better than, because you feel less than. You are not able to accept yourself where you are and allow others to be where they are. Then, you are not capable of real love. Real love is an unselfish concern that freely accepts others and seeks their good.

The truth of the matter is no one ever really possesses anything anyway. You may have use of it for a time, but it's only for the present. Items are lost, cars wrecked, houses sold. No one can be sure for how long you will be blessed with either a possession or a person's presence.

## HAPPINESS

*Happiness is*
*a juicy big orange*
*sand covered tennies*
*beaches and sunshine*

*Happiness is*
*the giggles of children*
*their enthusiasm for life*
*our love for them.*

*Happiness is*
*quiet calm waters*
*warm rays of sunshine*
*the giant great redwoods.*

B eing in envy is, as the definition says, painful. One way out is to let go. Another is to accept what you have as being enough. Let go of complaining about what you haven't had in the past. You can never go back. And don't worry about what you might not have in the future. You won't know about the future until you get there!

When you notice yourself feeling envy, you can use this as an opportunity to model. For example, I know a twenty-two year old woman who is gifted with both beauty and multiple talents. Older women think she is precocious; that her deep wisdom is wasted on someone so young! They could, instead, look at her as a wonderful model for living, loving and learning. They could transform the energy they are putting into envy into new vistas of self-growth, giving themselves permission to be magnificent, outrageous and beautiful.

The negative feeling of envy can be turned into something positive if you can use your own awareness of another's pre-eminence to transform your thought patterns! "Since you've done it, I can too!"

**119**

By skipping the resentment and pain, by not needing to bring others down in order to elevate ourselves, you can transform your envy into our magnificence.

> We see clearly
> when our actions are clean and to the point.

# CONTROL AND FOCUS

Control comes from trying to get what you want when you want it. Control implies authority, directives and tension. Control means on your time schedule and no one else's!

Usually, control involves a power struggle, which is really a struggle with yourself, a "no-win" situation. And with control comes the possibility of loss of control—to your own illusions or to the person or situation you are trying to control. Control says you can win if you argue long and loud enough. Or believing, if you just keep doing the same thing over and over again, next time things will be different. Needing control usually involves a little stubbornness too!

The truth is, all you can do is *try* to have control. You never really do. You set yourself up with behaviors which harm and ultimately destroy you.

The Serenity Prayer, used in many 12 step programs, is one of the best I know for surrendering control of people, places and things:

*"God grant me the serenity to accept*
*the things I cannot change,*
*the courage to change the things I can,*
*and the wisdom to know the difference."*

Focus, on the other hand, implies an awareness of the task at hand. A willingness to get the job done and a commitment to doing it! I like to focus on flowing with the river, instead of swimming upstream.

When you are focused, your boundaries and those of others are clear. You can approach the situation with integrity and ethics. Move forward with purpose. You are on target.

# Chapter 12

# Abundance

*Decision Making*
*Abundance of Time*
*Slow Down*
*Abundance of Money*

> Accept where you are now—
> otherwise, you negate yourself
> and what you're doing.

What does abundance look like for you? Assess your priorities and then decide: Are you open to having your life look different?

People with an abundance of energy are intent—they move forward with intent. They might be skiing or working on the side of the road with a pick-axe, but they radiate health and life.

They have learned to move out of emotion into motion, out of scarcity into abundance. There is a movement, a shift, a transformation.

*I am not always aware of abundance. Sometimes I deliberately put myself into spiritual, emotional or physical self-deprivation in order to gain an awareness of the way I live.*

*This may take the form of a cleansing fast. This allows me to reconsider how I want to feed and nourish my body. It may be a holiday; a retreat, perhaps, that allows me to examine my work role. It may be letting go of relationships. It's okay to have what's exactly right or nothing at all.*

### LIFE WITH EASE IS...

*...walking at your own pace.*
*...listening to your heart instead of your head.*
*...letting go of stress and tension in the only way you know how.*
*...smiling and saying hello if you want to.*
*...getting up early to watch the sun rise, or sleeping in and awakening to life.*
*...wearing what is comfortable and what makes you feel great.*
*...letting it be okay to change your mind after you've made a commitment.*
*...looking to see what works for you.*
*...enjoying the grace and beauty of two swans.*
*...being focused and moving forward at a brisk pace. And most of all—*
*...recognition and acceptance of the idea that life with ease is okay for you and for me.*

---

Once you have decided, don't look back.
What was there
may no longer be an option.

---

## Decision Making

If you are having difficulty making a decision, look carefully at what is stopping you from being decisive. Could it be you haven't gathered enough data in order to make a clear, concise decision?

What more would it take to be clear? Look inside.

**123**

*I am at peace. I am still. I have many choices about what to do next with this day, this moment. I will live it as if it is my last, knowing and accepting the consequences of tasks uncompleted. I will strive for balance—first things first—with simplicity and ease. I will focus my efforts and abilities on areas that are pertinent to the path that I am on.*

Ask yourself, "What do I have at stake in not allowing my life to have Excellence with Ease, Power with Passion, Prosperity with Play?"

### LETTING GO

*The colored leaves shimmered*
*A dance so delicate and delightful.*
*It was as if they were saying "I'm ready. The time has come."*
*It was as if a gentle, quiet spirit was hanging out in the giant tree.*
*The twirling, twisting leaves, remembrances of the long*

*summer, were saying farewell and bidding adieu to the past.*
*It was time for revitalization, rest.*
*Time to simplify, time to focus on what is next for the magnificence which belongs only to this tree,*
*to rebuild, restore and again burst forth in vivid emeralds—*
*the purpose of which is shade, security and safety for God's creatures, and a source of breath for all.*

---

Abundance of time becomes a reality
if we say it is a reality.

---

# ABUNDANCE OF TIME

To realize an abundance of time, we must live in the present.

**124**

✤ Each task not completed burns energy until the task is completed or scratched off the list.

✤ Do each project one at a time. This allows focus and completion.

✤ Avoid being overwhelmed; always remember you are what you say you are. If you say you are confused, you are. If you say you are focused, you are.

✤ Commit. Goethe said, "Until one is committed, there is hesitancy, the chance to draw back, always ineffectiveness." So ask yourself, "Am I committed?"

✤ Remember you have a choice.

✤ Complete for a new beginning.

✤ Stay within your integrity. If you are unhappy or angry, do what needs to be done to free yourself.

✤ Look at your well being. Are you rested? Have you had too much food or not enough? Too much exercise or not enough? Too much activity or not enough? (We're a bit like tires. A little bump puts us out of balance, then we need alignment.) It's okay! That's what life and living look like!

✤ Risk! Go out and do what you say you will do! Movement away from "business as usual" takes all-out risk. After all, life is but a daring adventure, day after day.

Many of you have lived most of your years hurrying from project to project, activity to activity; searching for knowledge, and wisdom. You want to experience everything, explore every avenue. You forget to take a time out. You forget to stop moving. You forget to feel. You forget who you are.

**125**

Time can be either abundant or scarce. Time is defined by you and you can choose abundance!

### THE ENEMY

*Is time the enemy?*
*Or is it our frantic attempts to control time?*
*Or is it the intensity*
*With which we sometimes insist*
*On managing ourselves?*
*Being present in each moment*
*Means a total surrender to the universe:*
*An admission of powerlessness*
*Over any wild, frenzied frantic issues of control*
*Of the moment.*

---

I am the source of my experience.

---

# SLOW DOWN

*On a visit to a beautiful Japanese garden I took a moment to sit on a small wooden bridge. The view was lovely with lotus blossoms, a tinkling stream, giant kois and water lilies.*

*Many people passed quickly through the two-acre garden, missing the experience. The subtlety with which everything had been laid out provided a feast for the senses. Hundreds of views were provided by standing in a slightly different spot, of looking in a slightly different direction.*

*They missed the care with which the trees were groomed, the delicacy of the training of the branches. They took pictures, but did not allow the experience to become indelibly imprinted on their minds. The pictures ensured memories for later, but what about now?*

Consider an ocean sunset. How often have you watched an entire sunset, right through to the dark of night, just for the sake of enjoying the ever-changing display of color? It is in these places, at these times you can ask philosophical questions—and get the answers.

This seems to be an all too familiar metaphor for living life: "How quickly can I get through this without experiencing it?" You wait instead! Wait for the right job, the ideal spouse, until the kids are out of diapers, until they're in school, until retirement! You can "wait" yourself right into your grave.

Is it time to slow down? Observe the infinite beauty close at hand. Even tiny steps will lead to your final destination.

You *can* choose to experience today now, in the present. And you can own your experiences, knowing that "the now I am in" is not necessarily "the now you are in" and that's okay.

## MELODY OF LIFE

*Sometimes fast, sometimes slow*
*Sometimes happy, sometimes sad—*
*The harmony is there just waiting to be heard.*
*What would it take to stop for a moment*
*And listen, really listen*
*to the sounds of the night*
*the sounds of the day*
*the sounds of dusk*
*the sounds of dawn*
*For in these quiet moments you will hear*
*The Melody of Life.*

> We have an abundance of money
> when we accept that we have enough.

## ABUNDANCE OF MONEY

If you are in a "financial bind," you can examine your options and simplify your life. You can choose to not spend in excess of your earnings. You can choose to let go of anything taking money that may not be essential. This might be a life-insurance policy, furniture that is being kept in storage for a later date, a larger than necessary home or too many dinners out at fancy restaurants.

You must be willing to have abundance and to recognize it for what it is—enough. You can shift from thinking in terms of scarcity into action and acceptance.

# Chapter 13

# NEEDS

*Needs*
*Boundaries*
*Setting Boundaries*
*Owning Power*
*Grieving and Acceptance*

> Acknowledge your feelings;
> honor your body;
> listen to its subtle messages.

## NEEDS

I t is important to choose your words carefully when you say what you need, want or desire. You may use "need" when you mean "want". "I need a bigger office," "I need more money," "I need an assistant," "I need to..."

Needs are those things that keep you alive and growing as a human being. "Wants" or "desires," on the other hand, are those things you might decide you would like to have to improve your quality of life.

> Boundaries include
> knowing who you are
> and what you are willing
> or not willing to compromise.

# BOUNDARIES

Personal boundaries are set by each individual. Yet in a society which has been taught to please, this can be a most difficult task. You may wonder if you will still be liked, or in some cases loved, if you can define your limits.

When there is boundary violation, body movement is constricted, muscles are tense, breathing becomes shallow and joy is not present.

When your personal boundaries are violated, you set yourself up for a slow death. Yet in your personal and business life how many times in one day do you allow yourself to become a victim?

How often have you gone home from work wondering what life is all about? Perhaps you feel you have no life outside your job and your family commitments. And yet you don't quit. It's back to the office, the phone calls, the visits.

Your business can often become your downfall. It's called burn-out. You feel the heat of transactions. You listen to the needs, wants and demands of others. You continue to give more and more of yourself until there is nothing left to give.

The body knows what it needs and will tell you, if you are willing to listen. But often you don't listen. You push on until there is nothing left for either your business or for your families and (most important of all) for yourelf.

I like to equate life to a Christmas tree and our energy to a beautiful string of lights. As you let your boundaries be violated and continue to please others at the expense of yourself, you lose lights. One light at a time dies. There is no warning. It just loses it's life.

Each time you abuse your body, mind or spirit by not listening to the subtle internal messages, the beautiful lights on the tree go out, one by one. At first you don't even notice you are missing a light. In fact it takes many burned out lights before the string gets any attention.

All of a sudden the tree is not quite as bright. The room is not quite as well lit and a little of the magic, the sparkle, is missing.

Little by little, important parts of who you are, the parts that have made you so special, so well liked, so well loved, are no longer present.

It's not so much that you change, but rather, you give up who you are. You no longer are the same sparkling person who so energetically did the work and basked in the glory of a job well done! But you are tough! You smile as long as you are on the job! The moment you climb into the privacy of your vehicle, the smile leaves your face and your concentration is funnelled into survival.

You have no patience for other drivers. You ignore the sights available to you on the drive home. You just want to be home so you can relax from the pressures of the job.

After arriving at home the "demands" of the family, which may be simple requests, now become an incredible burden. During the day too many of your lights have been flickering and now threaten to go out. Still you keep going. It's not yet time to quit. Keep moving, keep running, get the phone call, hold the kid, feed the dog, water the grass.

Whew! It will be wonderful when you go on vacation. It will be wonderful when the kids go for a visit with grandma. It will be wonderful when you can sleep in.

Yes, it will be wonderful when you sit down and read the newspaper, a trade journal or, heaven forbid, a novel! It will be wonderful when...

### REMEMBER

*Remember who you are*
*Remember why you are here*
*Remember: All you have is the moment;*
*All you have to give is love.*

*Be gentle with yourself*
*Be gentle with other souls*
*For only when you love yourself*
*Can you fully love others.*

*To be present—*
*To listen, to hear the quiet time*
*Is when you feel and remember*
*How insignificant you are in the universe,*
*Yet how complete*
*And whole you are*
*Within your own private world,*
*Your world within.*

*You make a difference*
*By who you are,*
*Your smile, your heart,*
*Your love, your light.*

*Remember who you are.*
*Remember why you are here.*

> When we feel vulnerable to others,
> perhaps our barriers are down.

# SETTING BOUNDARIES

In setting your boundaries, it helps to have a "Not to Do" list. If you overwhelm yourself with "To Do's" your energy drains and you become more vulnerable. Monitor your energy! Simplify! Eliminate! Do only what is in your focus and for the moment. Listen to your heart.

It's okay...

❖ to give to yourself, to love yourself.

❖ for things to be okay.

❖ to be a little lonely.

❖ to be quiet.

❖ to hurt.

❖ for your mind to chatter.

❖ to have fun.

❖ to be with people different from you—that's all there is: people being with people.

And keep in mind:

❖ It takes all of you to be you—do not rob yourself of yourself.

❖ When you are in a mood, the only one that can move you out, is you.

❖ You can choose to laugh or cry, sing or complain.

❖ You can have a willingness to be present to each moment, to see the opening for serenity.

✤ Your tap root is love.

✤ The more you can love yourself, the more love you have to give to others.

✤ Feel the silent pulse—each person is the universe.

✤ Let the door open a crack and look at the light beaming through.

What are your boundaries in relationships with others? In relationship with yourself?

Try this. Draw a large circle on a white sheet of paper. This represents your boundaries.

Consider those situations and feelings you desire to have in your life such as love, healthy relationships, music. Whatever makes you feel whole and complete, include inside the circle.

Next, list those situations and feelings that make you feel uncomfortable, bad, belittled, or violated. These may include verbal abuse from a colleague or a superior, an unwanted visit from a relative, gossip, addictive substances. Put these outside the circle.

Pretend the circle is your body. You have defined what is acceptable in your life.

You have also defined those things that are not acceptable If a person or situation presents any of these, be honest with them and with yourself. Let those around you know your boundaries.

### RESPECT

*How would it be*
*If each human was aware*
*Of all other humans?*
*How would it be*
*If each cell in our body*
*Was respected by the human organism inhabiting the body?*

**134**

*How would we look in relationship*
*If we were to function as one soul?*
*And if we were as aware*
*Of the effect of each human entity*
*As we were of our own cellular make-up?*
*The answer is found*
*In the quiet essence of self.*

---

You have the answer within you.

---

# OWNING POWER

Look back at your circle. How can you deal with those things you wish to keep out of your life to make sure they stay out?

There are a couple of phrases I've found effective:

"It doesn't work for me."

If something is not right, then say so, without making anyone, including yourself, wrong. Know "It doesn't work," and acknowledge it.

"Let me think about it."

Weigh out the costs and benefits in terms of time, energy and money. This stops you from reacting on impulse. This focuses the proposal time and allows you to think about it. It sounds so simple, yet it is not easy to own your own power.

Richard Bach writes, "No one can solve problems for someone whose problem is that they don't want problems solved."

**135**

> Learn from each experience.

# GRIEVING AND ACCEPTANCE

### TEARS

*Tears are the soul's way*
*Of cleansing and healing.*
*Let them be.*
*Just as the leaves of the trees*
*Glisten with freshness after rain,*
*So, too, does the soul shimmer with luminance*
*Reflecting wholeness, peace and joy.*

As you let go of anything, you grieve, you miss what you had. When you acknowledge the sadness, it then begins to slowly dissipate.

If you have looked at your situation from only one perspective, shift to the other extreme and see what it looks like from there. It's like viewing San Francisco from a skyscraper and then getting the feel from the sidewalk. The grieving process is very much a part of acceptance. When you accept this is the way it is—the office, the family, yourself—then you give up the illusion that "It will be better when...". Power comes from accepting what *is* and letting it be. Accept the rain today or the 108° temperature or the frost that killed your favorite bougainvillea. Grieve your losses. Feel the sadness.

Kahlil Gibran wrote in The Prophet, "Your joy is your sorrow unmasked."

Acceptance is being able to see and accept whatever is so for you at the moment. Acceptance brings with it an ability to be comfortable enough, now.

**136**

You can deny where you are: "I really don't believe this beautiful day!" "Can you believe this traffic?" "I can't believe you'd do something like that!" But denying only stops you from really accepting life as it is. It keeps you in a fantasy world, a world of delusion and illusion.

*I accept that I change my mind a lot. I don't make choices easily because I feel pinned down. The choices I do make are made because that's what is important at the moment. They are subject to immediate change if they cease to work for me.*

You maybe find it difficult to take responsibility for your own decisions. Perhaps you want someone to shoulder the responsibility so you don't have to make decisions. Let go of the idea that anyone else can make decisions for your life and accept who you are.

### ONE

*Things aren't working, control ebbs*
*Frantic—running faster, faster, faster*

*When the momentum peaks*
*One is catapulted into a new territory*
*Soon you discover*
*You don't belong where you are*

*If you stay too long*
*Dis-ease transposes into disease*
*The path becomes narrower*
*Choices fewer and fewer*

*Your pace also quickens*
*Evolution and transition occur*
*In a blink of an eye, as if by magic or miracle*
*And you realize Life is as it is*
*With no beginning, only the center*
*And something beyond an end.*
*Anger, resentment, frustration*
*Honor them, acknowledge them*

*Trust that's it's okay to let feelings go*
*They are not who you are*
*You cannot control them*
*They control who you are*

*They are the darkness*
*They are the suffering*
*They are the tragedy of life*

*Let go—Let grow*
*Let life be so*
*Let there be light*
*Let there be life*

*We are but one*
*We are the all*
*You are in me*
*I am in you*

*We live—We die*
*The Seasons come—the Seasons go*
*To all an end—To all a beginning*

*PART 6*

# THE CONTINUATION OF CHANGE

**Chapter 14**
**THE CONTINUUM**

# Chapter 14

# The Continuum

> Today, I will be totally truthful to myself, as
> never before.

Change is constant. It's like the wind. There is always movement, be it ever so slight. It's when we ride into the wind that the going gets rough.

*I remember recently going out for a morning bike ride on a windy day. I rode for a few miles into the country. I had calculated the direction of the wind to be from my side. I traveled with ease, and I felt confident the return ride would be as easy.*

*As I began the homeward trip, the wind became more powerful and dirt from the newly plowed fields was blowing with gusto across the road. Unfortunately, the wind was now head on and riding became nearly impossible.*

*I called on every bit of strength I had, at one time getting off the bike and walking alongside it! I felt silly. My muscles ached. I wanted to stop! But... I knew I had the strength to get through this rough spot.*

So often life is lived riding into the wind—*Excellence with Ease* forgotten—*Power with Passion* forgotten—and *Prosperity with Play* forgotten.

*My past had been filled with excellence, power and prosperity. Learning to incorporate the ease, passion and play was another challenge. I am constantly awakening to new ways of bringing ease into my life; new awareness of how I ride into the wind in my relationships with myself, my family, and the world.*

*Now I celebrate the "Ah ha's!" and it feels wonderful! I welcome with an open heart the windows that allow me to see clearly to the other side. The windows that give me options, choices. The windows that will open to a new way of living, giving me what I asked for when I climbed Devil's Tower: Excellence with Ease, Power with Passion, and Prosperity with Play.*

You must be like the Aikido Master and learn to recover quickly as you make mistakes. That's what the Paradigm for Change does. It allows us to become aware, willing, committed, risk-takers, and trusting in order for us to again see our choices.

People ask me, "Where are you now on the mountain called life?" Let me tell you, I am still climbing, and the top is nowhere to be seen! I now have the tools, the knowledge, the strength and the faith to climb and climb and climb.

I have a support system that keeps me going. I have learned to recognize what it is I want. As I share my visions and dreams openly with others around me, it's almost as if they're guaranteed to come true! And my dreams and visions are coming true! Miracles do happen on a daily basis!

I'd like to address some questions frequently asked in my workshops and presentations.

**Do new changes get any easier or less painful?**

*For me, the changes become easier only because I accept the movement or change sooner. The mountain trail becomes steeper as what I have at stake becomes greater. The pain is present. I've*

**141**

*just learned to soften to it, to breathe and relax. What I've released is the suffering. As Stephen Levine has said so beautifully, "Pain is real, suffering is chosen."*

**Do I still have to grieve?**

*Whenever our life changes, (whether it is a child growing up and no longer needing us as before, or a parent growing older and not being capable of caring for themselves as they once did, or moving to a new home or apartment), we feel the pain of change. Yes, I feel the loss of what once was. I cry. I feel and grieve the loss. However, how long I cry and grieve are entirely dependent on how ready I am to get on with my life. I can choose to some extent the length and depth of my feelings. I find it easier to go to the depth of the well and go through the feelings instead of being in a large lake of shallow water, wallowing and wallowing.*

**Does each stage in the paradigm get easier?**

*No. Each stage has it's own set of challenges. Each stage has incorporated in it all the other stages, ad infinitum. It's a matter of being willing for our lives to be different.*

**Do I always have to start a new cycle blind or asleep?**

*If you can see clearly and you are fully awake, you will not have any new awarenesses. You will already know.*

**If I set my vision for being "on purpose", how do I know my choice is right?**

*This is the time to quiet your mind and listen and feel. How does your body feel with your choice? You will know the answer and your decisions will not require any explanation, reasons or justifications for them to be right or wrong.*

**I have just moved my life out of the danger zone and into the comfort zone. Why should I keep taking risks, and must I?**

*Sometimes you need a "time out" from taking risks. Trust yourself to know the answer. For me, I keep taking risks. I take risks in telling my truth as it is for me each day, in relationships with myself, others and the world. As I accept, love, honor, serve and become one with all, I am constantly on the edge. The paradigm is always present. When will I quit? That's the beginning of the dying process.*

**In order to stay fully alive, do I need a vision?**

*I can't answer this question for anyone else but myself. I find having a vision, with the intention to implement it into my life within a five-year period, keeps me on target. It allows me to focus on what is really important. It allows me to know which star to aim for and keeps me in tune with what is happening in my life that is congruent or incongruent with my vision.*

**How do I know to really trust what you say about abundance? That I have enough Time, Energy and Money when I say I have enough?**

*You can only trust yourself. What I am saying is nothing new. I am only saying what has been said for centuries before. I've just said it in my own words, with my personal experiences. The theory of increase (money for example),—when you give and tithe it will come back to you—doesn't necessarily mean it will come back in the same form (money or material matter). If the money you spend on your taxes is spent with resentment and anger, then what you have increased in the world is anger and resentment. If you spend your time watching a small child and it brings you joy and satisfaction, the increase in the world will be joy and satisfaction. It doesn't make much sense to me to increase anything other than joy, play, fun, sharing, love, acceptance and other such energies. It's only when you say you have enough, that you have enough.*

**What's the next step?**

*"To be a star, you must shine your own light, follow your own path, and don't worry about the darkness, for that is when stars shine brightest!"*

Anonymous

### GROWING

*Take time to be quiet
To feel, to integrate
We move quickly through life
Telling all, Sharing all
Yet we let go of the good things
The warm fuzzies, the cozy feelings.*

*Take time to be quiet
To go nowhere, have no purpose
Take time to anchor wonderful moments
In your life.*

*Let your body feel
Let your body remember
All the old ugly things
Share them—and release them forever.*

*Consider warm memories—
Hold them close
Only then can you share
So that others too may grow.*

It's time to acknowledge the life force pulsating through our veins. If you cap your creative forces, anger and rage appear as demon volcanoes. Anger is then inappropriate to the situation. Through creating, whether it be music, art or sports, you allow the life force to flow through our bodies. You release emotions and move into motion—the ACTION step.

**144**

The benefits of releasing anger in an appropriate manner—punching pillows, running, shouting—create an incredibly beautiful calm. The mind is quiet, the soul peaceful.

---

Judgements we have about ourselves
allow others to have the same judgement.

---

You see, in the long run, it doesn't matter if you have money and material possessions. Even though some have and some don't have, we are all human beings, worthy of love, respect and hope.

It's easy to become overwhelmed by helpless feelings when you think about world conditions and inequities within your country, state and city.

Just remember, as you heal yourself, you heal your family, your country and your world. Who you are does make a difference.

Wealth comes in many forms. It begins with an awareness and appreciation of ourselves. From there it can grow and grow. Keep taking tiny steps! Keep reaching out! Keep saying:

"Yes! Yes! Yes to life!"

"Yes to love!"

"Yes to friends!"

### THE FALL CHILD

*I felt like a child, I became a child*
*It started out as an early morning walk.*
*The autumn sky was pink and violet*
*With only a few wispy clouds*

*I walked along the streets of my home*
*I tried to see the horizon but it was hidden*
*Big houses, manicured lawns, stately trees*
*Blocked the view where land meets sky*

*Then appeared a peek of the breaking of early morn*
*The sun was calling and I couldn't push down my excitement*
*I found a vacant lot and ventured on,*
*Down the irrigation ditch, up the irrigation ditch*
*Tall weeds, cattails, spider webs, loose dirt and bugs*

*I plowed through without a thought or concern*
*All of a sudden I was standing in a freshly plowed field*
*Witnessing the daybreak without interference*
*It was beautiful! I was awe struck by my freedom*
*Magically appearing simultaneously with the birth of the new*
*day*

*I looked down at my pale pastel clothing and smiled*
*Cobwebs, dirt, berry stains, and seeds clung to my clothing*
*I remembered my sons in their younger days*
*And experienced some of the pleasure they surely felt*
*In the woods, at the river, and over the levy*

*I walked on experiencing for the first time*
*The joy of being nowhere and going nowhere*
*I pick a twig abundant with berries*
*And placed it next to my skin on my chest*
*I felt the cool vibration of life*

*The sun rose quickly and soon I saw my shadow*
*It was big and tall and graceful and beautiful*
*I walked with it and shared a communion or two*
*The earth beneath my feet and my body became one*
*I felt the presence of my child and my children*

*I felt the presence of all children, all life*
*Tears welled up and I realized the life all about me.*
*I was aware of each minute particle of life*

**146**

*I saw the flatness of the place I had called home*
*For nearly three decades and I knew*

*Without question it is time to move on*
*To give up and let go of all I thought was*
*To go back to nature, from where I came*
*Away from what had been my safe haven*
*Away from those who had been my strength*

*There comes a time in each of our lives*
*Where what has been, no longer is*
*And it is time to head for the hills and the sea*
*To be just what it is that God meant it to be*
*A life for me with thee.*


*IN THE MIDST OF MY DARKNESS,*
*I FOUND THE SUN*
*WITHIN MYSELF*
                        Camus

# Recommended Reading

Bach, Richard. *Jonathan Livingston Seagull; Illusions: The Adventures of a Reluctant Messiah, The Bridge Across Forever, One*

Berkus, Rusty. *Appearances: Clearings Through the Masks of Our Existence*

Blanchard, Kenneth, PhD. & Johnson, Spencer, M.D. *The One-Minute Manager*

Bowden, Judy & Gravitz, Herbert. *Genesis: Spirituality in Recovery From Childhood Traumas*

Burgett, Gordon. *Empire Building by Writing and Speaking*

Carnegie, Dale. *How to Stop Worrying and Start Living*

Cornell, Joseph. *Listening to Nature: How to Deepen Your Awareness of Nature; Sharing the Joy of Nature: Nature Activities for All Ages*

Covey, Stephen R. *The 7 Habits of Highly Effective People*

Dyer, Dr. Wayne W. *You'll See It When You Believe It: The Way to Your Personal Tranformation*

Earll, Bob. *I Got Tired of Pretending*

Foundation for Inner Peace. *A Course in Miracles*

Dawain, Shakti. *Living in the Light: A Guide to Personal and Planetary Transformation*

Gilbran, Kahil. *The Prophet*

Hay, Louise, L. *You Can Heal Your life*

Heider, John. *The Tao of Leadership: Lao Tao Te Ching Adapted for a New Age*

**149**

Hesse, Herman. *Siddhartha*

Jeffers, Susan, PhD. *Feel the Fear and Do It Anyway*

Keen, Sam. *Fire in the Belly: On Being a Man*

Levine, Stephen. *Who Dies? An Investigation of Conscious Living and Conscious Dying*

Mandino, Og. *The Greatest Saleman in the World; The Greatest Secret in the World; The Greatest Miracle in the World*

Natsbitt, John & Aburdene, Patricia. *Megatrends 2000: Ten New Directions for the 1990s*

Parry, Danaan. *Warriors of the Heart*

Peale, Norman Cincent. *The Power of Positive Thinking*

Peters, Thomas J. & Waterman, Robert H., Jr. *In Search of Excellence: Lessons from America's Best-Run Companies*

Rodegast, Pat & Stanton, Judith Ed. *Emmanuel's Book II: The Choice for Love*

Roman, Sanaya. *Personal Power Through Awareness*

Schultz, Suan Polls Ed. *Reach Out for Your Dreams; Don't Ever Give Up Your Dreams*

Siegel, Bernie S. M.D. *Love, Medicine & Miracles: Lessons Learned About Self-Healing from a Surgeon's Experience with Exceptional Patients*

Smotherman, Ron M.D. *Winning Through Enlightenment*

Vissel, Barry M. D. & Vissel, Joyce. *The Shared Heart: Relationship Initiations & Celebrations*

Waitley, Dr. Denis. *The Psychology of Winning: Ten Qualities of a Total Winner*

Walters, J. Donald. *The Art of Supportive Leadership: A Practical Handbook for People in Positions of Responsibility*

Williamson, Marianne. *A Return to Love: Reflections on the Principles of A Course in Miracles*

Wollam, Ray H. *On Choosing—With a Quiet Mind*

Zukav, Gary. *The Seat of the Soul*

# ABOUT THE AUTHOR

From waiting tables at her parent's diner in the Black Hills of South Dakota to the creation and co-ownership of one of the most successful real estate brokerages in suburban Sacramento, Shirley Summer now lives the realization of her own vision.

Shirley's expertise in coaching businesses and businessfolk to reach their full potential by helping them create their vision, and intermediate plan of action, has now spanned 15 years and a half-dozen formats: workshops, speeches, retreats, books, group or team consulting, and one-on-one counseling. Among her clients are corporations, small businesses, national associations, academic institutions, academic insitutions, government entities, and individuals.

She is a member of The American Society of Trainers and Developers and the National Speakers Association. She is a Certified Real Estate Broker Manager in the Realtors National Marketing Institute, and is an active board member of the UCDMC Sacramento Hospice. Shirley now shares her formula for success in her book *COURAGE TO CHANGE*.